How To Succeed at
SKATING

How To Succeed At

SKATING

Monika Maier

STERLING PUBLISHING CO., INC. NEW YORK

First published in the United States of America in 1982 by Sterling Publishing Co., Inc., Two Park Avenue, New York, NY 10016

Translated from the German by Beverley Worthington

© BLV Verlagsgesellschaft mbH, Munich 1979

First published in Great Britain by
Orbis Publishing Limited, London 1982

All rights reserved. No part of this publication may be reproduced, stored in a retrieval system, or transmitted, in any form or by any means, electronic, mechanical, photocopying, recording or otherwise, without the prior permission of the publishers. Such permission, if granted, is subject to a fee depending on the nature of the use.

ISBN: 0-8069-4154-5

Printed in Singapore

Contents

Introduction 6
Equipment 8
Clothing 10
Basic terms 12
Skating school I 16
   Skating forwards 18
   Skating backwards 30
   Turning 41
Skating school II 50
   Jumps 51
   Spins 58
   Curve skating 68
Ice dancing 77
   Dance holds 77
   Dancing Three 80
   Mohawk 82
   Choctaw 84
Dances 86
   Glide waltz 86
   Fourteen 88
   Kilian 92
Information on free skating 96
   Building up a free
     programme 96
   Short programme 98
   Free skating classes 99
   The most common jumps 100
   Skating school I
     programme 102
   Skating school II
     programme 103
Information on compulsory skating 104
   Compulsory figures 109
Information on ice dancing 114
Information on pair skating 119
Rules and marking 122
Between two winters 125
Glossary of terms 126

Ice skating is a sport that involves travelling over ice using skates. The skater's weight is borne by the narrow blade of the skate. This causes enormous pressure on the surface of the ice below, a thin layer of which then melts and the ice becomes smooth enough to enable the skater to glide easily over it. The melted ice acts like oil, reducing friction. As soon as the skate has passed over a section of ice, the melted snow immediately freezes again.

In flat areas of country, ice skating has become particularly widespread as an alternative to skiing. Today both old and young can make the most of a fine winter's day on the ice. But in the 18th century everything was quite different. Then ice skating was considered most unsuitable for adults and was only tolerated among children. Figure skating was not possible either at this time. To begin with, people skated with the help of long wooden runners, which were curved at the front and had a steel blade inserted in them to act as a sliding surface. They were fastened to boots with straps. With these, you could cover mile after mile of countryside that had first flooded and then frozen, particularly in flat areas like Holland and northern Germany.

Then ice skating developed various disciplines, such as ice

speed skating, ice hockey and figure skating, which includes free and compulsory skating, pair skating and ice dancing.

Since ice skating offers many variations and something for each age group, it is an ideal family sport and a change for stay-at-home people, since it can mean getting out into the fresh air.

No special exercises are necessary as preparation. Only the really rusty bones need a bit of 'oiling' to lessen muscle aches and pains that would otherwise deter you from skating. People who have been on hikes or extended walks well into the autumn, for example, are well-prepared for the ice-skating season. In winter, visits to an ice rink should be just as frequent as seeking out an indoor swimming pool. Both these types of sport complement one another ideally.

Equipment

Ice hockey boots

Speed skating boots

Figure skating boots

Considerations before buying

It is very important to think before buying the necessary equipment, since there are many facets to ice skating. If you are keen on the fast sport of ice hockey, you should choose suitable ice hockey equipment with padded boots reaching above the ankles. The blades of the skates are specially made of sheet steel rounded off at the front. You steer yourself by means of a flat, hollow-ground blade.

You also need ankle-high boots for speed skating, for which the blades can be up to 40cm (or 16in) long. These are made of tubular steel with a recessed edge. If you like speed, this is the equipment you should choose.

The main feature of skates used for figure skating is the hollow-ground blade. This is necessary for moving forward over the ice and particularly important for skating clean figures. The blade has an inner and outer edge. The boots are almost calf-length and have an ankle guard around the instep. You should test the skates regularly by running your thumb lightly over the blade to make sure you can feel both edges. If you can feel only one edge, you must get the blade sharpened straight away. Your sports shop

Equipment

Testing the blade

or an expert at the ice rink or stadium will do this for you. You can also ask an expert to fit the hollow-ground blades to skates. You need not worry about fitting instructions since ready fitted skates can be bought in sports shops and the sports departments of large stores.

Safety considerations

Under no circumstances should boots be bought to be grown into, since boots that are too large can cause many problems when you skate using the edges of the blade. There is also a danger of straining the muscles of the feet. But if you take good care of your boots and skates you can easily sell them again – at second-hand shops, for example.

When thinking about buying, you should also bear in mind the aspects of safety on the ice and take what precautions you can. Skaters using the almost calf-length figure-skating boots will have the best grip (regardless of age or the type of skating activity).

Tip
Beginners should therefore play ice hockey in figure-skating boots. Later, when they are steadier on the ice, they can graduate to specialized skates.

Young children can at the beginning use gliders or double runners to help them get accustomed to the ice. Gliders have broad blades fastened underneath tough boots and prevent skaters from wobbling or stumbling.

Even the smallest children can move around the rink safely with gliders.

Clothing

As with all kinds of winter sports, you should not wear lightweight clothes for ice skating, otherwise your muscles will not be protected and you could injure yourself in a fall. Long, warm trousers with legs as tight as possible are recommended. Pullovers that allow the upper part of the body unlimited freedom of movement are suitable to complete your skating wear. Of course, sufficiently stretchy ski suits are also practical. As far as possible, young skaters should be protected against the cold by cosy ski suits. On the whole they move about very carefully and soon get tired; and when their limbs get cold, they quickly lose interest in skating. Of course, there are also skating jerseys. But with them it is absolutely necessary to wear warmer tights. Skating jerseys are very suitable for free skating, but are rather limiting when doing compulsory figures. Gloves should be worn for compulsory figure skating, since the whole arm movement can become stiff and clumsy if you fingers are numb. Thin, woollen socks are an advantage since they absorb sweat better than socks made of synthetic material. Heat accumulates inside the tough boots and thus the soles of the feet can become unpleasantly hot.

Preparations at home

You should certainly try on new skates several times at home (keeping the covers on, of course). This way you can break in the boots. Gradually try to achieve a crouching position, by springing up and down and bending your knees, until the boots no longer press at the instep.

Important
Do not cheat by lacing up the boots too loosely. If the boots are made with an additional eye at the top after the last hook, then you must pull the laces through this as well. This will substantially improve the position of the foot.

Types of games

Unlike skiing, there are no skating nurseries at ice rinks. Nevertheless the smallest children can enjoy the ice and take part in a family sport. Gliders have already been mentioned, on which children slip rather than slide; these are not only safe but also allow freedom of movement. Dressed in cosy ski suits, young skaters can be kept warm and happy playing a host of games with or without grown-ups.

To overcome initial shyness and uncertainty, some games are

Young skaters

Learning to skate by playing games and being entrusted with blades rather than gliders.

particularly suitable, which small children have already learned from older brothers and sisters or from nursery school, perhaps. These include such things as 'cat and mouse'. Proper ice skating can often be furthered by games of this sort.

Arrange a slalom run by placing gloves, scarves or small heaps of snow on the ice as markers. Go round each marker in increasingly narrower arcs and with more and more momentum. The up-and-coming skaters will soon find out that by crouching lower the arcs can be skated more easily.

Let the children make a snake. The skaters should stand in a row according to size and hold on to the waist of the person in front with both hands. Firstly skate in large curves at a moderate speed and then tighter circles and even figures of eight. Then everyone should try to slow down by crouching.

Even a competitive game such as an 'egg and spoon' race can improve your child's control on the ice. And if a prize is offered as well . . .

Basic terms

Axis Long axis of the ice rink (or ice surface); this is the imaginary straight line that divides the ice into two halves lengthwise.

Barrier Closing off of the ice surface with a railing. This term is also used in this book to mean the outer edge of the ice.

Centre of circle The imaginary centre of the ice, also called the middle of the circle.

Closed position The arm and pivot leg, either left or right, go in the same direction.

Counter-direction The direction you are skating on the ice when moving clockwise.

Counter-position The arm on the side opposite the pivot leg points forward into the circle. The counter-position helps with balance.

Curves Half-circles, whole circles or just sections of a circle.

Direction of travel The direction generally preferred on ice rinks, which is counter-clockwise.

Free foot Foot not on the ice.

The skating foot is pointed outwards on to the ice.

Outside position.

Basic terms

Free leg The leg not on the ice.

Inside The weight of the body is put on the inner edge of the skate.

Open position The direction of travel is either forwards or backwards; keep arms to the sides at hip height with palms towards the ice.

Outside The weight of the body is put on the outer edge of the skate.

Sequence of steps Sequence of steps from which a dance is put together.

Skating foot The foot on the ice.

Inside position

Closed position = initial stance.

Open position = leading up to it.

Basic terms

Skating leg The leg on the ice.

Step Often not only the movement of a foot but frequently the usual expression for certain combinations. It is the visible trace on the ice made by one foot. It can consist of curves or turns with sections of curves.

Tension The pull that results when the shoulder blades are pressed back with one arm pressed firmly in front and one pressed firmly back.

Turn out When the free foot is held forwards or backwards, the toe always points outwards on to the ice or away from the body.

Abbreviations

R	= right	Ch	= Chassé
L	= left	T	= Three
F	= forwards	Sw	= swinging movement of free leg
B	= backwards		
O	= outside	Mo	= Mohawk
I	= inside	oMo	= open Mohawk
X	= crossed	Cho	= Choctaw
FX	= crossed in front	oCho	= open Choctaw
BX	= crossed behind	~	= quick change of edge
Dt	= double-time		

Skating school I

Loosening exercises for warming up.

First steps on the ice

If your initial attempts at skating are on a natural ice surface, you must first of all make sure that there are no signs on the banks of the pond or lake prohibiting you going on to the ice.

Before taking off your skate guards at the barrier, warm up with a loosening exercise: stand with the legs slightly apart and move both arms forwards to shoulder height; now swing them back, at the same time squatting down and then straightening up; then swing your arms back to the front again, while bending your knees and straightening up again. Repeat this simple exercise five times.

This should be enough to loosen your muscles and lessen the risk of falling.

Important
Relaxed, loose leg and arm positions are the most important requirements for safe movement on ice.

Balancing on two runners – the basic position

It is particularly important when first coming into contact with the ice that you incline the upper part of the body slightly forwards and that you bend your legs loosely at the knees. You must never stand on the ice with your knees straight. If you do, the main weight of the body is too far back,

Skating school I

You should stretch your muscles to improve agility on the ice.

pressure on your heels increases and your skates start moving forward. The net result will be your first bodily contact with the ice.

Technique
To be able to keep your balance, hold your arms slightly bent to your sides at hip height, always keeping the palms facing down to the ice.

Especially important for balance: starting position.

Skating school I

Correct helper's position.

Avoid leaning backwards at all costs.

1. Skating straight ahead

If there is no-one on the spot to help you make your first attempts on the ice, you must adopt the initial position (as described on page 17) with particular care. But if you find someone to help (it is not necessary for the person concerned to be on skates), he or she can give you support in the following way. It is best if your helper stands on the left and, using the right hand, holds your arm on the inside of the wrist. The left hand supports you underneath the left elbow. In this position, using some help, take care that you stand to the side a little and in front of the person helping. If for any reason you get into a backwards position, you can still be lightly supported. Also the skater's position can be controlled better in this way and, if necessary, he or she can be reminded that the upper part of the body should be forwards.

Mistakes

At all costs you must avoid clinging on for support and waiting to be pulled. You will then be stretching out both arms for help and this will soon put you in a backward position, resulting in the inevitable fall.

Skating forwards

Technique
Each step begins from the closed position, ie both feet close together. With the first movement, bend both legs slightly, resting your weight mainly on your left leg. Now shift your weight on to your right foot, turning it slightly outwards on the ice; with your knees bent, give a strong push away in the direction of the barrier. Since the weight of your body is resting on your right leg, the resulting pressure is on the outer edge of the skate. You have then reached the outstretched position

As you pushed with the right foot, you slightly raised the free left leg off the ice and pointed it backwards with the foot turned out. As you stretch out your right leg, you pull the free left foot up from behind. With the leg slightly turned out and with the knee bent, you then bring down the left foot in the direction of the middle of the circle, using a push. Stretch the skating leg out again. Bring the left foot up from behind to begin the next step; lower it with the skate turned out slightly and the knee bent once again in the direction of the barrier.

To start with the steps will be quick and short, scarcely giving the idea of gliding. But with each new push there is more flow and sweep in the movement.

Important
You should always make the push with the skating leg turned out. If you bring your foot down straight, the toe rakes (picks) at the front end of your skates will cut into the ice and break the momentum; you will thus lose your balance and almost certainly end up on the ice.

2. Crossing over

You are normally restricted by the area available for ice skating. Maybe an open-air rink has not been cleared of snow and you have had to sweep some of it away yourself; it won't be long before you reach the edge. Since ice skating consists totally of flowing movements, there are no sharp angles or edges, but gentle transitions and curves only made possible by putting weight on the inner edge of the skate.

Technique
After the last straight step counter-clockwise, you must shift your weight from the outer edge of the left foot to the inner edge of the right foot. This movement also involves a change in arm position or in the whole of the upper part of the body. If you keep your arms by your sides and your head straight, you will be looking into the middle of the circle in the curve. Move your left arm back with the left shoulder

Skating school I

slightly inclined into the circle – lower down than the outer right one. Keep your right arm forwards in the direction you are going. After you have finished the curve, take your arms back to the sides.

If you start the steps from the closed position, while standing on the left outer edge, bring the free right leg closely forward past the skating leg and bring it down in the direction you are going, crossing it in front of the left leg. Keep your knee bent and your foot turning slightly inwards. This should leave the trace of a rounded-off curve on the ice.

Bring the left leg (now the free leg) up at the side from behind and then down, turning it slightly outwards just in front of the skating right foot (towards the middle of the circle).

This cross-over is the beginning of a curve that is the first requirement for almost all figures. At the beginning these steps, taken inwards on the right leg, will be very short.

But if you always start out with your knee bent and skate out the curve until the skating leg has straightened, you will get momentum; slowly you begin to glide. In the counter-direction, therefore opposite to your usual direction, make the same movements in the opposite way. Make the last straight step on your right leg.

The cross-over.

Summary

Bring your free left leg up past the other – then down, crossing it in front of your skating right leg turned slightly inwards. Start the open outward step on the right leg. Right arm behind – shoulder lower – left arm and left shoulder forwards in direction of travel.

Skating forwards

Tips and types of exercise
The cross-over is used not just for curves; it also allows you to skate whole circles on the ice. It is even more interesting if, after crossing over in the circle, you try it in a figure of eight, making two circles next to one another while dividing the ice in half. At the so-called cross-over you change position, your arms alternating slowly and steadily, never jerking. You may be surprised to learn that you have a definite favourite side and a direction you prefer in which you find it much easier to carry out movements. This is even more noticeable when doing jumps and spins.

It is therefore advisable to practise the sequences of movements in **Skating School I** really intensively on both sides (usual direction and counter-direction). Moreover this gives you the advantage of opening up many more possibilities for variations in ice skating later on.

3. Double-time step

Whereas when skating straight you bring the free leg down from the closed position, with double-time you bring your free leg gently past your skating leg and place it on the ice. Your skating leg is now your free leg; lift it off the ice in the track of the new skating leg.

Double-time step

Technique
If you have started the last step on the left outwards towards the middle of the circle, now bring your free right leg gently past your skating leg and put it down, also in the direction of the middle of the circle but without shifting your weight to the inner edge; this way you will be skating in a curve. Afterwards bring your free left leg up from behind and gently past your skating leg, setting it down once again towards the middle of the circle. It is equally possible to carry out this sequence of movements towards the barrier as well. Then make sure your head always looks in the direction of the point of your skate on the ice. Keep your arms by your sides at hip height. The double-time step of course starts from the knee. Just before straightening up fully, begin the next step so that the low-high movement is not too exaggerated.

Skating school I

4. Change step

Here you get to know a combination of steps in which the length of the individual step is of great importance. To work out the rhythm more easily, you should count out: one, two, three – four.

Technique
The first step starts in towards the middle of the circle on the left foot. Keep your arms at your sides with your head looking in the appropriate direction. Then gently bring your free right leg past the skating leg and down in the track left by the left skating leg. Bring the left leg (now free) gently from behind to the front and once again set it down on the ice in the track of the right skating leg. You are now standing left forward outside and have made three short steps towards the middle of the circle (left, right, left). Pull your right leg (now free) up to the left skating leg and move it towards the barrier from the closed position. Hold this fourth step for noticeably longer and keep your knee well bent until your skating leg is fully straightened.

Then once more take three short double-time steps into the middle of the circle, followed by a long drawn-out outside step to the right towards the barrier.

5. Chassé

The step that follows now is very similar to the previous one. You must take special care when moving your free leg and bringing it down on to the ice. For a change start off for once by going towards the barrier, also counter-clockwise of course.

Technique
Keep your hands and arms by your sides at hip height, with your head facing in a counter-clockwise direction. With the first step, therefore, you go forwards to the right and outwards. Pull up your free left leg from behind and quickly bring it down directly parallel to your skating leg. Do not move your free leg (now the right one) backwards, but lift it quickly off the ice, with your knee slightly bent, and bring it quickly down again on to the ice to the right forwards and outwards towards the barrier. Now your free left leg is well stretched out behind and only afterwards moves up to the skating leg.

Important
With the Chassé, the emphasis is on the right foot as it holds the gliding movement for a relatively long time. You can also skate the same Chassé towards the middle of the circle.

Skating forwards

Chassé: you only just lift your free foot off the ice.

Step crossed in front.

Summary

Bring down on left, forwards and outwards – bring down on right parallel – raise free left foot little way off ice and bring it down again right away.

This time, therefore, the emphasis of the Chassé is on the left foot. Using this step you can string together as many passages as you like, either in one direction only or alternately in both directions.

6. Cross step

Now there only remains the cross step to complete the forward steps. This step has many variations. First of all, try it crossed in front. A double-time step is the starting point for this.

Technique

Bring down your left foot forwards into the middle of the circle. Bring up your free right leg and move it on past to cross it over in front, bringing it down right next to the outer edge of the other leg's skate. Make sure in all this that your knee is markedly bent and your left shin and right calf are close together. The cross step becomes much easier if you keep your free and skating legs well bent. Afterwards, bring your left leg (now the free one) up next to the right skating leg from behind and set it down outside towards the middle of the circle, again with your knee sharply bent.

Skating school I

Skate this step until you are fully straightened up. Then try doing the same to the other side, towards the barrier.

Summary

Bring up free left leg from behind – cross in front and bring it down – skating and free legs well bent – move free right leg from behind up next to skating left leg and bring down outwards.

You can also skate this cross step crossed behind. Again start off from a double-time step.

Technique
Bring down your left foot forward outside towards the middle of the circle. This time cross your free right leg behind and bring it down by the outer edge of your other foot's skate. In so doing, you bring your left calf and right shin firmly together with the knees bent. Crossing behind is made much easier if you keep both the skating and free legs well bent during this passage. Lift your left leg (which is now free) off the ice, move it gently forward over your skating right leg and bring it down next to it in a closed position outside. At this point you can vary the rhythm again by holding the crossed-behind step for longer. For this you must stay down considerably longer on your knee before straightening up to begin a new step. You can also skate this step up to the barrier.

Summary

Skating leg right towards barrier – free left leg brought down crossed behind – skating leg straightened – move free right leg to front over left skating foot – bring down beside it right outside in closed position – straighten up.

Skating forwards

7. Camel

After you have mastered the basic essential steps for moving forward on the ice, you can now try your first small figure. Its success depends on a little body control.

Preliminary practice
After a short run-up, start with a step forward on either leg; hold it for a long time. Keep your free leg stretched out behind, but a bit higher than you usually do. Keep your arms by your side but at shoulder height. Pull your shoulder blades back for this and keep your head well held up.

Technique
Bring down your skating leg from a position with the knee well bent and keep your arms and shoulders as previously described. Stretch out your free leg fully with the foot turned outwards (point your toes to the side and upwards) and move it behind and upwards until it can be held level with your head and shoulders. Take care to lift up your free leg from behind and not from the side. This would be easier, but makes balance difficult and looks unsightly.

Beside initial bangs on the head, this figure also involves a lot of muscle aches and pains. Learning and mastery of the camel can be made much easier if you do some preliminary work at the barrier.

Practice exercise
Stand with your face to the barrier holding on in front with your arms stretched out to the rail. Bend your skating leg slightly, stretch out your free leg with as much spring as possible and swing it up behind with your free foot turned out. At each swing you will bob up and down a lot. Then try this exercise with your skating leg straight. But you must always take care to keep your head straight to the front and your shoulders parallel to the ice. Otherwise the upper part of your body will turn to the side towards your free leg, which is stretched up, and it will be impossible for you to keep your balance.

Tips
- With these gymnastics you must of course watch out that other skaters are not inconvenienced.
- If there is no barrier available for this exercise or you don't want to do any 'gymnastics' on the ice, you can work out just as well at home. You only need an armchair or the edge of a table that is not too low to support your arms.
- Here, too, it is worth holding your head up and pressing back your shoulder blades.

Skating school I

Forward camel in open position.

Camel while standing at the barrier.

Gradually spread your arms out further in the standing position until they are at right angles to your skating and free legs. You should only then try to do this figure on the ice with a swinging movement. When you feel safe enough skating this straight, you should begin to skate the camel during a circle.

Camel outside
You need another arm and shoulder position for this. If you move counter-clockwise first, practise the camel forwards and outside on your left foot. Here you don't take up a counter-position, but an open position.

Technique
Stand on your skating leg, with the knee slightly bent. Move your left arm forwards but do not keep it at shoulder height. Make a line with your slightly bent lower arm and your thigh. Your shoulder should then point into the circle. Your head too should look towards the middle of the circle. Stretch your right arm back and up until it forms a line with your left arm in front.

If you find that your best side is on the right leg, skate in the opposite direction.

Summary
Skating leg bent right outside – right arm in front – right shoulder leans into circle – left arm behind – keep free left leg horizontal and turned out.

Skating forwards

Camel forward outside.

Camel forward inside.

Camel inside

You can also skate a camel inside. But this requires greater body tension.

Technique

To skate a camel inside in the counter-clockwise direction, stand on your right leg with the knee slightly bent. Keep your left arm slightly bent in front with the back of the hand at the height of your right thigh. Stretch your right arm out high behind. Keep your left shoulder lower and incline it slightly into the circle. Make sure your head also looks inside the circle over your shoulder. Hold your free left leg stretched out at head height with the foot turned outwards to form an imaginary line again.

Summary

for opposite direction:

> Skating leg bent left inside – right arm in front – head looks into circle – keep free right foot level and turned out.

Skating forwards

8. Moon

This figure is skated in a round shape, giving it its name. Move counter-clockwise and stand slightly inwards on the right leg.

Technique
Bring your free left leg up from behind closely past your bent skating leg and forwards. Point your right arm forwards and keep the left one behind. Now stretch your free foot in a flat curve just above the ice. Then, with the point of your skate turned out, bring it up to the track of your skating right leg and put it down. Then straighten both legs. Keep your arms by your side at hip height, with the upper part of your body now facing into the middle of the circle. Move over the ice with your legs apart and turned outwards. This position should be well-known from gymnastic lessons.

Summary
for the opposite direction:

Left inwards in counter-position – move free right leg, turned out from behind, past bent skating foot to front – put right foot down in track of left skating foot – straighten up.

Skating school I

Starting to turn.

Shifting weight on to the left leg.

Pulling up the free right leg to the skating left leg.

1. Turning round

When you can skate forwards using a whole range of steps and sequences, it is time to learn how to move backwards. To do this, you must first be able to turn round.

Technique
Skate forwards counter-clockwise, with your arms at the side at hip height, shifting your weight markedly on to your right leg. Turn out your left leg until the tip of your skate points backwards. But do not lift your foot off the ice. Guide it gently over the ice, putting most of the pressure on the front part of the blade. Now you should be standing parallel to the barrier, hips in the open position, ie the point of your right foot pointing forwards, while the left points backwards. Of course your heels should not come together or form an angle of 180°. Ideally your skates should form a slight curve. Then shift your body weight on to your left leg, with the knee bent, so that you are facing backwards. Lift your free leg (now the right one) quickly off the ice in passing and bring it up to your left foot in the closed position. Now you have achieved the starting point for all following backward steps.

Skating backwards

Tips
- Even when skating backwards it is absolutely necessary to watch that the upper part of your body leans markedly forwards to avoid falling over. Your head should form an imaginary line with your bent knee.
- If you are not wholly successful turning round, you must make sure just before turning that there is enough room available to practise.
- When starting to skate backwards never forget to glance over your shoulder so that you can take evasive action at the right time or stop, even when concentrating hard on the next steps. Skaters who come up from behind should also consider other skaters.
- To get a feeling for moving backwards, from which you will be able to develop backward gliding, you should stand at the barrier with your back to the centre of the circle.

Initial position for skating backwards.

Glancing over your shoulder.

Skating school I

2. Pushing off backwards

Preliminary practice: pushing off on two feet

Hold on to the rail firmly with both hands and try to push off with your knees pressed together and your legs bent. When your knees touch on the inside, your heels move outwards. On the other hand, both sets of toes turn inwards so that you almost get into an X-leg position. Make sure that your back, when stretched out, forms a line with the heels of your skates. Now push off with your knees and the tips of your skates at the same time, keeping your legs well bent. Your weight is on the inner edge of the skate. This means each foot sketches out a slight curve inside. Slowly straighten up again and try to get your feet once again into a closed position. In the meantime you will have moved off from the barrier and can begin to push off a second time.

Technique

Stand upright in the closed position and press together the inside of your knees and your toes, while turning your heels outwards. Your weight presses on the runner edges of your skates, making a slight curve inwards. Then straighten up and pull your skates back into the closed position.

To hold your balance, keep your arms bent at the side at hip height, your palms parallel to the ice. At the first attempts you will only get a little momentum from pushing off. Once you have started gently with this parallel pushing-off, you can begin the second step.

Pushing off on one foot

Again stand in the closed position with your arms at hip height by your side.

Pushing off backwards from the barrier.

1 & 2 *Pushing off: weight on inner edges and knees bent.*
3   *Straightening up, closing feet together and*
4   *back into the initial position.*

Skating backwards

Skating backwards

Technique
This time only bend your right knee slightly inwards towards your other knee and let your right leg take most of your weight, shifting the pressure on to the skate's outer edge. Push your left foot (turned outwards) forward over the ice, lift it slightly and bring it back to the skating leg. Then bring it down parallel to the skating right foot while you straighten up slowly. This time, even when starting off, turn your left knee slightly inwards and press off with your bent knee. Then turn your right foot outwards and push forward over the ice; you can even lift it briefly off the ice. Move your free leg (now the right one) back to your skating leg as you straighten up slowly and set down your right foot close to your skating foot.

Summary
> Pushing off backwards right backward outside – right arm back – left leg pushed forward – left arm in the front – pull up free left leg until parallel – arms at side – pushing off backwards on the left backwards and outwards – left arm back – right leg pushed forward – right arm in front – pull up free right leg until parallel – arms at side.

3. Changing over

From practising the forward steps you will know that changing over has to be mastered before tackling curves and circles. When you have to an extent mastered the backward push-off with momentum, stand on the right leg backwards and outwards for the initial position.

Technique
Keep your right arm back and lean your shoulder into the circle. Your left arm points forward. Hold your head looking slightly over your right shoulder into the middle of the circle. Push your left foot forward on the ice. Then lift it up and cross it over your right skating foot until your knees touch. With the knee bent, put your free left leg down in front of your skating right foot, but to the side. Then give a powerful kick backwards with your free leg (now the right one) until it is stretched out with the point of the other foot turned out. Pull your free right foot up at the knee and set it down in the closed position, while straightening it up slowly.

1 & 2 On the left foot backwards and outwards.
3 & 4 Push right foot forward and gently cross it over your skating foot.
5 & 6 Weight on right foot, lift your left foot off the ice behind.

Skating school I

Now push your left foot gently forward over the ice again and lift it up. Cross it over the right skating foot so that your knees press together and, with the knees bent, bring it down in front of the right skating foot and a little to the side. Now you are standing on your left leg backwards and inwards. Give a powerful kick behind with your free leg (now the right one) until you have stretched it out completely with the toes turned out. Then bring it up from behind your skating leg, which is still bent, and put it down next to it in the closed position. Meanwhile slowly straighten up from the knee. Also try out the change-over in the same way on the other side in the opposite direction.

Summary
for the opposite direction:

 Initial position on left leg backwards and outwards – left arm behind – head over left shoulder towards inside of circle – right arm in front – lift right foot up a little in front and cross over left skating foot – set it down to the side in front, with knee bent – position right backward inside – straighten – kick back with free left leg – bring up to skating right leg and put down in closed position – straighten.

Bring your free leg up past the skating foot . . .

4. Change step

Move backwards over the ice in a counter-clockwise direction with the long axis in front of you. After the last step with the left leg, put down your right foot outwards towards the middle of the circle.

Technique
For this keep your arms bent by your side at hip height. Your head should look into the circle slightly over the right shoulder, which should be inclined a little bit lower. Bring your free left foot from the front closely past your skating foot and then put it down in its track, also towards the middle of the circle. Lift your right foot off the ice and move it from the front closely past your skating left leg and put it down behind outside in its track.

Now bring your free left leg from the front as far as your skating leg and then, with your knee bent and turned inwards, give a good kick left backward outside towards the barrier. Your

... and put it down in its track.

left shoulder is lower for this and your head now faces the barrier.

Bring up your free right foot from the front to the closed position and then put it down outside towards the centre of the circle. Incline your right shoulder a little lower and make sure your head faces the centre of the circle. Now bring your free left leg from the front closely past your skating foot and set it down in its track behind. Then bring your free leg (now the right one) also from the front closely past your skating foot and once again set it down outside in its track. While doing so, straighten up from the knee, bring your free left leg right up to your right foot and turn your head to the barrier. Again bend at the knee and kick off outside in the direction of the barrier, turning your left knee slightly inwards. Hold this step for a bit longer until you have slowly straightened up from the knee and are able to pull your free right foot from the front again.

Now try out the change step in the same way to the other side.

Skating backwards

For this you must not skate 'against the current', but you can skate on further in a counter-clockwise direction.

Summary

Initial position on right leg backward outside – put down left foot outwards to the barrier – left arm lower down – head inclined to barrier over left shoulder – lift free right foot from ice – put down right behind skating leg in its track – lift free left foot off ice in front – put it down just behind right skate in its track – straighten up – bring free right foot up to skating leg to closed position.

Kick off on right leg outwards to middle of circle with knee bent and turned inwards – lower your right arm – head inclined into circle over right shoulder – hold step longer and pull up free left leg to closed position.

Practice exercise
You can link these change steps to one another while skating three double-time steps to the barrier and then three double-time steps to the middle of the circle. Head and arm positions are exactly the same as for the 'pure' change steps.

Skating school I

5. Chassé

This step requires particularly neat footwork since your skates must be placed as closely as possible or closed on the ice. It will help if you can maintain a well-controlled body position for this. Bend loosely at the knee, keeping your arms to the side at hip height and your head straight. In this position your head, fully stretched back, and the skate on your skating leg should form a line. To check it, look in the mirror at home and see if your position is correct.

Technique
Skate backwards counter-clockwise and finally stand on your left leg. Using your right foot, give a good kick into the middle of the circle with the aid of your knee turned slightly inwards. Pull up your free left leg from the front right up to your skating foot, only putting it down briefly on the ice. Keep your free leg (now the right one) right by your skating leg in the closed position and only just lift it off the ice (roughly up to the ankle of your left skating foot). Immediately afterwards put it down right backward outside once again, parallel to your left foot with the knee bent. Push your free left foot briefly forwards over the ice and only pull it up to your skating leg when straightening up.

You can also begin the Chassé going towards the barrier.

Skating backwards

4 5 6

Summary

First step backwards on left leg outside – pull up free right leg from front – put down close to other leg – lift free left leg just off ice – immediately put down again – pull up free right leg from front and straighten up.

Tip

- In the Chassé you get momentum from the first and third outside steps, in which you get more power by kicking with the knee turned inwards slightly.
- The Chassé can be skated alternately into the middle of the circle and towards the barrier. But then watch out for your arm positions. In spite of keeping your arms by the side, whereby your head is always inclined over your shoulder counter-clockwise, when going to the barrier your left arm should be held a bit lower; when going into the middle of the circle, your right arm should be held a bit lower. Initially this makes the shifts in weight easier when you are not used to them.

1 Initial position LBO (on left leg backward outside)
2 Bring up right leg; bring down in closed position.
3 Lift left leg just off the ice briefly.
4 Put it down again right away.
5 Bend your knees.
6 Give a good kick LBO.

Skating backwards

6. Cross step

Out of the backwards steps there only remains the cross step, crossing in front or behind. But since the 'pure' cross step only occurs in ice dancing, we shall be content here in **Skating School I** with just a few variations of this step, which can be skated as linking steps or in so-called transitions.

For example, you can link a crossed step to a backwards Chassé (right, left, right).

Technique

Bring the free left leg past the skating right leg, then set it down crossed slightly behind by the outer edge of the right leg's skate. With the knee well bent give a good kick by lifting up your free leg (now the right one) and thereby skate towards the barrier in a left backward outside curve. Hold your free right leg low over the ice in front with your toes turned out. In this backwards curve bring your right arm well behind, while keeping your left arm in front, rather lower and parallel to your free foot. Your head should look over your right shoulder. Afterwards bring your free right leg up next to the skating left leg and your arms into position at the side. After you have straightened up from the knee, you can add any step you like.

Practice exercise

You could skate a change step towards the barrier and adapt the last step (to the left, right, left, therefore the right outwards step to the middle of the circle). Then do not bring it down outwards in the closed position but crossed behind in the track of the skating left leg, also towards the barrier. This will result in an outward curve in which you hold your left leg in front. Afterwards cross your left foot in front over your skating foot and bring it down backward inside on the ice. Since you must make this step with your knee well bent, you can stretch out your free right leg behind. This will result in an inward curve. Only straighten up completely from the knee after this. Keep your arms to the side at hip height during these three double-time steps. Then, when crossing over behind, bring your right arm up to the front and keep it lower. Point your left arm behind, while your head looks over your left shoulder. Keep this position for the 'crossing in front' step too, but exaggerate it a little more.

Skating school I – Turning

Now you can move forwards and backwards reasonably safely and have reached the point when you should be able to change direction more and more naturally and from your momentum.

1. Moon turn

Remember that the first time we turned around, we made an uncontrolled curve with legs assuming a parallel position afterwards. Now we shall try the same thing while skating a moon turn. Here the precise shift of weight is, above all, important to achieve a flowing sequence of movements.

Technique
Change over forwards, going forwards counter-clockwise (left forward outside, right forward outside). Then right forward inside is the starting point for your turn. Shift your weight from the right leg forward inside to the left leg backward inside, with your face looking to the middle of the circle. This comes about as follows: stand on the right leg forward inside with your skating leg straight; pull up your free leg from behind until you can set it down without difficulty on the left backward inside to take your weight. You can then easily lift your right foot off the ice. Next bring your right leg close up next to it. Then you can continue skating backwards with a familiar change step or Chassé.

2. Loop

When changing over counter-clockwise, you change edges. After the last step (on right leg forward inside), put your left foot down forward inside, at the same time bringing your left arm forward and pulling your right arm back.

Technique
You should be facing the edge of the ice rink. Put your right foot down backwards and outwards to take your weight, while you lift your left foot gently off the ice. Then cross your left leg in front of your skating right foot. You are now standing on your left leg backward and inside. While facing the middle of the circle, put down your right foot forward inside. Your right shoulder should point in the direction you are going. You can then start your next loop or fit in a few double-time steps to link on.

3. Kilian step

The Kilian is made up of the beginning of the loop and the cross step. But the individual steps are shorter, ie the free leg is kept nearer the skating leg.

Technique
Once again the Kilian step starts off forwards in the counter-clockwise direction. Put your left foot down forward inside. Keep your left shoulder and left arm in the direction you are going and look towards the barrier. Shift your weight backwards and on to the right leg. Cross your left leg gently behind your right foot and lift your right leg (now the free one) off the ice, keeping it in front. Look into the circle, leaning your right shoulder down lower. The second part of the Kilian step starts with the change from left backward inside to right backward outside; bring your foot down in the closed position. Cross your left leg gently in front of your right foot and then put it down backward and inside. Finish the turn in the open position with a foot change to right forward inside.

Tip
- At the beginning you can try out these steps at home without skates or try them just standing on the ice. This is less complicated.
- When you have mastered the step reasonably well, try to divide it into two phases by counting deliberately. Hold the third step (left backward inside and right forward inside) rather longer. Build up a keen rhythm by stressing like this.

1-4 Crossing behind from RFO to LFI as an approach for the introduction.
5 Shift of weight to RO.
6 Left leg crosses behind.
7 Put down right leg next to it.
8 Cross left leg in front; change to RFI.

Skating school I

4. Three step

This is the first turn you can do completely on one foot. The name of this step comes from the mark left behind on the ice by the blade when doing the turn. In all sequences of movements, this turn should first be practised while standing on one spot. Body position plays a very important part in it.

Outside Three

Technique

Start with the Outside Three. For this, stand on your left leg and let your right shoulder and right arm point forward in the counter-clockwise direction. Keep your left arm behind, leaning your left shoulder into the middle of the circle. Press your right shoulder and right arm as far as possible into the middle of the rink so that your whole body turns too. Move your left shoulder and left arm back as far as possible until the turn has to be completed because of the extreme backward inside pressure emanating from this use of your shoulders.

Important

- You must take care not to shift too much weight on to the front of your foot and therefore on to the toe rakes (picks) of the skates or you will probably stumble over. This means that your weight should be spread evenly on the whole of your skating leg.

Preparation for a FO Three.

Using the shoulders at the beginning.

Turning

- When turning you should also take care that the free leg is able to perform a useful function. If, in fact, the free leg (here the right leg) is kept next to the skating leg in the closed position down to the knee and only the lower leg is bent slightly backwards, it is very much easier to keep your balance.
- After the resulting turn to backward inside, you can bring your free leg down on to the ice much more quickly and check more easily the considerable momentum from the action of the shoulders. Only then will your weight finally change on to your right leg and you are then standing on the right leg backward outside.

- You should carry out this sequence of movements firstly while standing and then several times without much momentum before trying out this turn at full pace. This will save painful contact with the ice.
- When you can turn with the Three when skating along – starting with knees bent to being straightened and the short turn with a change of skating leg from the left leg on to the right one, which is slightly bent – then your free leg is no longer bent in a cramped way during the turn, but held loosely behind.

You have mastered a very lively step when you have mastered the Three, the classic turn in a waltz on the ice.

After the turn.

Finishing it off.

Skating school I

Inside Three

Analagous with the Three from the left forward outside to the left backward inside, the Three from the right forward inside to the right backward outside is therefore skated with the turn starting inside. You should first practise the sequence of movements while standing, as in the first Three.

Technique

Stand on your right leg. Point your right shoulder and right arm forward and incline your left shoulder in to the middle of the circle. Hold your left arm out behind.

Press your right arm firmly into the circle, pulling your left arm back as far as possible. Again the turn comes about from this shoulder movement, but this time backward outside.

Proceed with your free leg as in the Three turning forward and outside. When you have completed the turn, you then change the skating leg, from the right backward outside to the left inside or change direction forward. Then skate the next step on the left leg forward outside.

1 Starting position FI.
2 Preparation for Three FI.
3 Start of shoulder movement.
4 After the turn.

Turning

5. Combination of steps

Using the steps and turns you have learned up till now, you can work out a considerable number of step sequences on the ice, which will enable you to venture towards your first combination of steps. It should then be easy to circle the ice rink using steps and turns in any order you wish. If you insert the steps you practised first, such as the double-time and change as well as the Chassé, between the individual turns you will achieve a considerable repertoire.

Here is an example to try out: begin on the long axis of the ice rink with several double-time steps, add two change steps (starting in towards the middle of

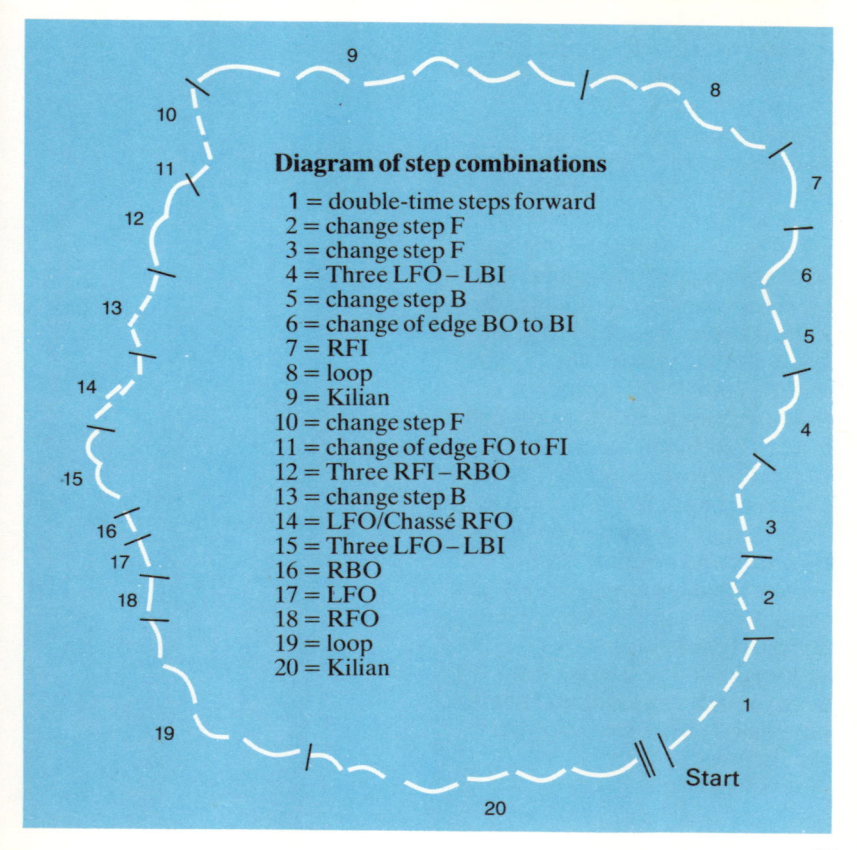

Diagram of step combinations

1 = double-time steps forward
2 = change step F
3 = change step F
4 = Three LFO – LBI
5 = change step B
6 = change of edge BO to BI
7 = RFI
8 = loop
9 = Kilian
10 = change step F
11 = change of edge FO to FI
12 = Three RFI – RBO
13 = change step B
14 = LFO/Chassé RFO
15 = Three LFO – LBI
16 = RBO
17 = LFO
18 = RFO
19 = loop
20 = Kilian

Turning

the circle) and follow them with a Three from left backward outside to left backward inside. Then comes a backward change step (also in the direction of the ice rink). By means of an easy change of edge, work out a left backward inside step from the last step left backward outside. By changing the direction of travel, you can easily add a right forward inside step to that.

Follow this with a loop and a Kilian step. You can link a change step to this particularly well. From the last right forward outside step the Three from right forward inside to right backward outside can be added on straight away by an easy change of edge, with a change step towards the barrier immediately afterwards. Follow this with a transition to left forward outside with a Chassé and another Three from left forward outside to left backward inside and change the skating leg to right backward outside. After another change in the direction of travel to left forward outside, link on a loop and a Kilian step.

(See the diagram on page 47.)

So, from your practising you are slowly developing free skating, almost a free section, even though you cannot yet build jumps and pirouettes into your repertoire.

Tips
If you get pleasure out of combining various steps, have a look at the ideas in the section on **Ice dancing**. But if you dream of planning your own free section, you should work on your ice-skating ability in **Skating School II**.

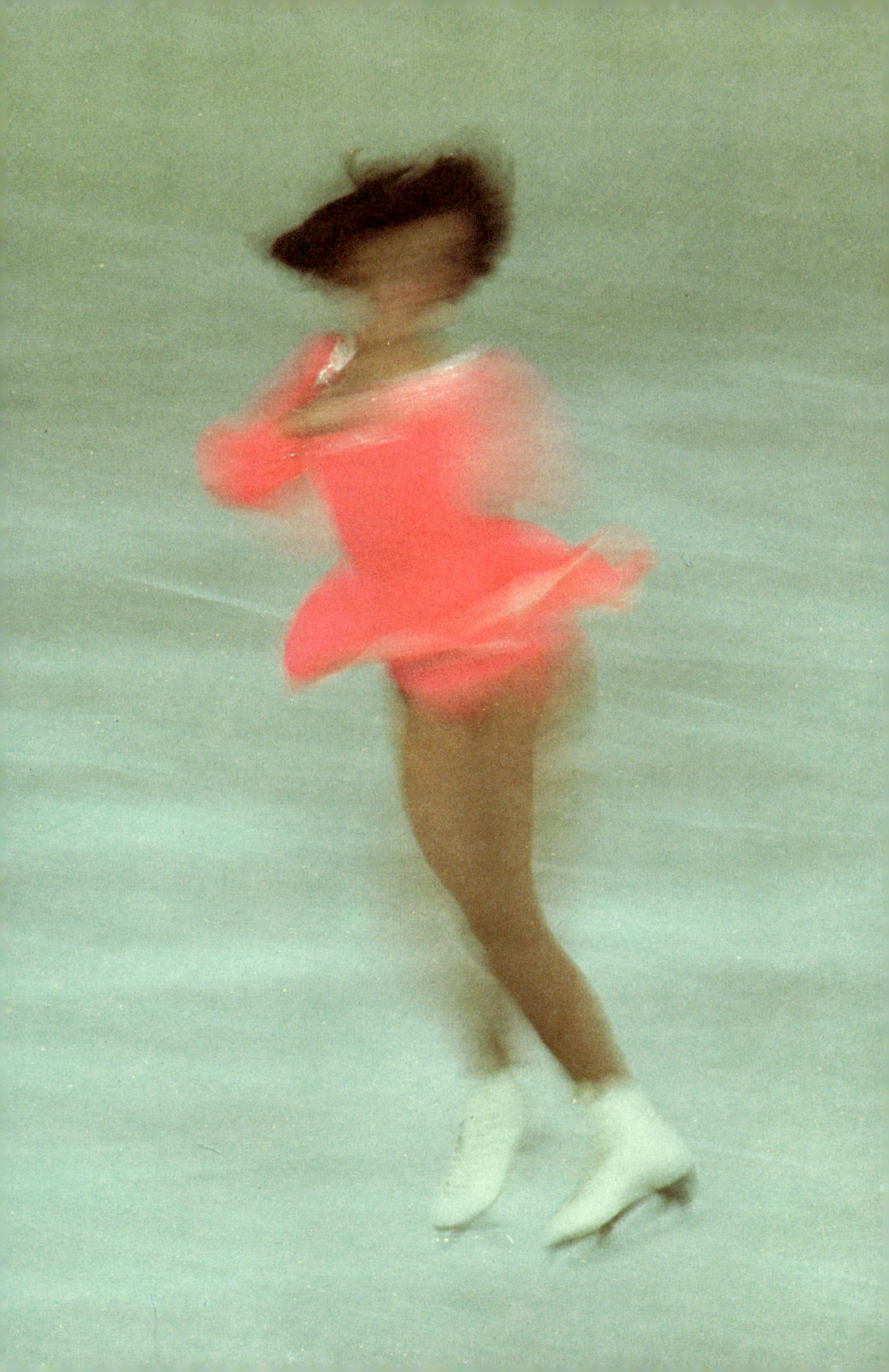

Skating school II

Since you can now move over the ice forwards and backwards safely, you ought to venture out and try your first jumps.

Each jump consists of three equally important stages:
- The start with the take-off.
- The turn itself
- The landing and finishing off.

Counter-position after landing.

Basic principles

For the take-off you must apply pressure on the jumping edge at the right moment, since you need some of your momentum to gain height. Jump up with your knee well bent and from a clean edge. There should not be any trace of braking or scratching of the toe rakes of your skate when taking off. The co-ordination between the movements of your arms, free leg and head is also important.

The axis of your body from head to torso should be as vertical as possible in the air. When you are in the air, you can only achieve the necessary momentum in the turn by closing your arms quickly – and, with some jumps, your legs too.

On landing, straighten out your arms and free leg as quickly as you can. This checks the speed of the turn and slightly enlarges the curve of your landing. The jump is also slowed down when you land gently on your knee. Keep your free leg stretched out behind. Straighten up slowly from your well bent knee. Here the correct arm positions play a large part in successfully avoiding 'overturning'. Otherwise you could make uncontrolled turns forward, thereby disturbing your balance.

Therefore when jumping up, you should keep your arms in the counter-position to support your balance. If you are standing on your right foot, point your free left leg behind and hold your left arm in front, slightly into the middle of the circle. Keep your right arm and right shoulder behind. You should be looking over your right shoulder into the circle with your eyes directed at the toes of your free leg.

Jumps

1. Hopping sideways

This is only a preliminary movement and not a jump in the proper sense.

Technique
Skate the last step left backward inside with your knee well bent.

Your head and body should be pointing into the middle of the circle. Keep your arms by the side at hip height. Keep your free right leg stretched out behind, with your free foot turned out. At this distance from the skating foot only the toe rakes (picks) should touch the ice and your knee

1 Take-off from toe rakes (picks) of left skate.

2 Landing on to toe rakes of right skate.

3 Closing legs.

4 Taking off again from toe rakes of left skate.

Skating school II

should be well bent too. Press off with the left skating leg. Then bring the left leg (now the free one) up and quickly straighten up. Immediately bend your knee again to gain momentum for the next take-off from the toe rakes of your left skate. Move your free right leg low over the ice and bring it down on the toe rakes of your skate. You can continue this sideways hopping for as long as you want.

Tip

However, you will achieve a flowing sequence of movements if you bring your left foot down on the ice, with the knee bent, with the whole blade of your skate forward inside after making three hops sideways. Take up a counter-position for this: skating leg left, left arm at the side behind, free right leg behind and right arm in front inclined rather lower down into the circle, so your head can look over this shoulder.

2. Tap jump

This is your first jump with spin, with which you move within an angle of not more than 180°.

Contrary to sideways hopping, this time your body does not go into the circle, but you look towards the barrier.

Technique

The initial step is right backward outside in the direction of travel. Point your right arm forwards and keep your left arm behind you. Look over your left shoulder. Stretch out your free left leg behind you, setting the toe rakes (picks) of your skate briefly on to the ice.

Important

The trick for this is not to tap your toe rakes on the ice with your foot turned inwards, but with your foot turned out so far that on contact with the ice it almost causes a forward movement. In this way both feet are on the ice and your knees are bent. Take off with both feet at the same time and close your legs during the jump, turning your whole body and your head until you have straightened up towards the barrier.

Now, going forward, put the toe rakes of your right skate on the ice and bring down your free left foot with the whole of the skate blade outside and the knee well bent. Keep your right arm behind and your left arm in front. Keep your head looking into the circle over your shoulder, which should be a bit lower than the other one.

Jumps

1 Use of toe rakes (picks) *LBI*.
3 Twist upper part of body further forward.

2 Close legs in the air.

4 Landing *LFO*.

Skating school II

3. Scissors jump

Technique

Start in exactly the same way as with a simple tap jump. Stand on your right foot backward outside in the direction of travel, keeping your free left leg stretched out behind and putting your toe rakes on the ice. Press your toe rakes into the ice with your foot turned out so far that you achieve forward movement with this crossed tap jump too. In this way the real spin occurs on the ice and not in the air.

When you take off with both knees bent, spin in the air with your whole body not only towards the barrier but try to twist the upper part of your body forward as far as possible. Just before the upper part of your body has completed a half-spin, kick your right leg forward past the left one (keeping it straight) and bring it back immediately to the left leg. Then bring it forward in a sawing movement. Immediately afterwards put the whole blade of your left skate down forward outside with your knee bent. Your left arm and head should then be forward in the direction of travel, with the right arm behind.

Jumps

4. Three jump

This gets its name from the mark made by your skating and free legs during take-off, turning and landing. It is one of the few jumps in which take-off can be directly forward. However, the approach for it is mostly backwards so that only the take-off itself is made forwards.

Technique

Skate backwards counter-clockwise and at the last stroke stand on your right leg outside with the knee bent. Hold your right arm slightly bent in front, while looking behind over your left shoulder, which should be dropped down. Move your left arm behind and keep it parallel to your free leg, which is stretched out behind and turned outwards. Then straighten your skating leg and pull up your free leg with the free foot turned outwards. Bring your left foot down forward outside with the knee well bent, lowering your left arm in front. Swing your free right leg further forwards a little to the side. At the same time press up firmly with your skating leg, ie spring up from the knee, using this movement for the take-off. Your whole body straightens up with your head facing towards the middle of the circle. It is particularly important to swing your arms up into an

3

1 After take-off from the toe rakes (picks), kick the right leg forward.
2 Close legs.
3 Landing LFO.

Tip

You can easily try out these tapped jumps at home without skates; as the name implies, contact with the ice should be light and brief. Right at the beginning it is very difficult to watch both your foot and arm positions at the same time, since both are involved in the same sequence of movements.

Practising this at home is at the same time a small lesson in gymnastics.

55

Jumps

open position when doing this.

Your free leg, which is still turned outwards and has traced a slight curve, now lands on the ice with the knee bent right backward outside. With these first attempts, you should try to land in a 'counter-position', that is with your left arm in front and your right arm behind, with your head facing into the circle over your lowered right shoulder. Keep your free left leg stretched out behind.

Important
- Naturally you should land on the whole blade and under no circumstances on the toe rakes, otherwise you could easily overbalance and fall flat on your face on the ice.
- You should also avoid overturning through using the 'counter-position'. Otherwise you would not be able to finish off the jump correctly backward outside with your knee bent, but would immediately have to turn forwards after landing and go off forwards out of control.

This Three jump is necessary preparation for learning the Axel-Paulsen jump later on. Skaters simply call it the 'Axel'. World-class skaters jump it three times, that is with three and a half revolutions (or 1260°).

However you should be satisfied if, after a bit of practice, you can finally tone down the counter-position, only keeping the corresponding right arm lower in front when landing. You should then be looking over your right shoulder into the middle of the circle.

This looks much more elegant and less novice-like. On the other hand, it also requires better body control, which can only be achieved after much practice and precise execution of the movements.

1 Changing direction from backwards to forwards.
2 Beginning of the Three jump.
3 Take-off LFO.
4 Swing free leg right forward.
5 High point of jump.
6 Open position when jumping.
7 Landing in counter-position RBO.
8 Finishing off.

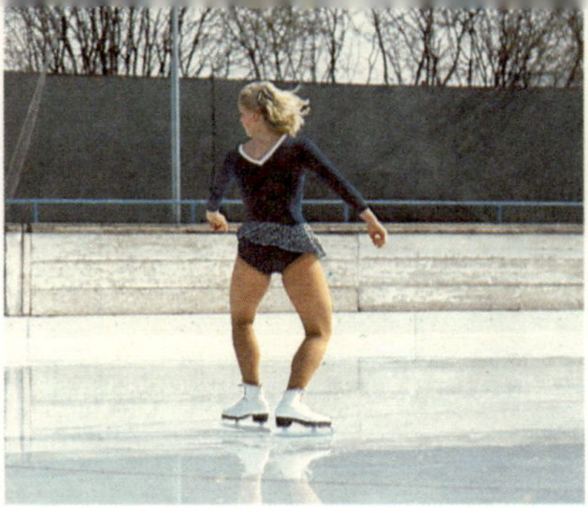
1

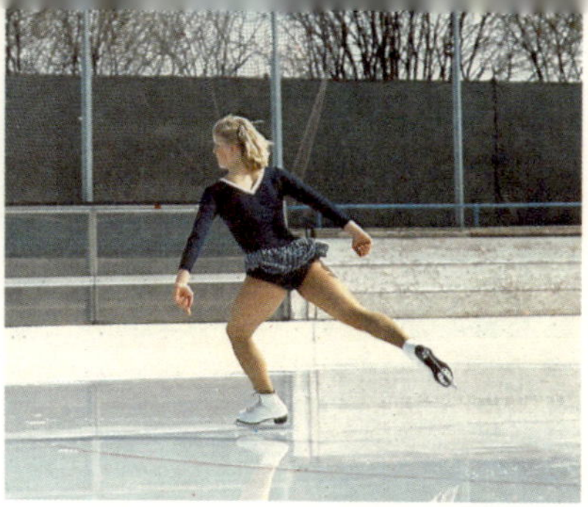
2

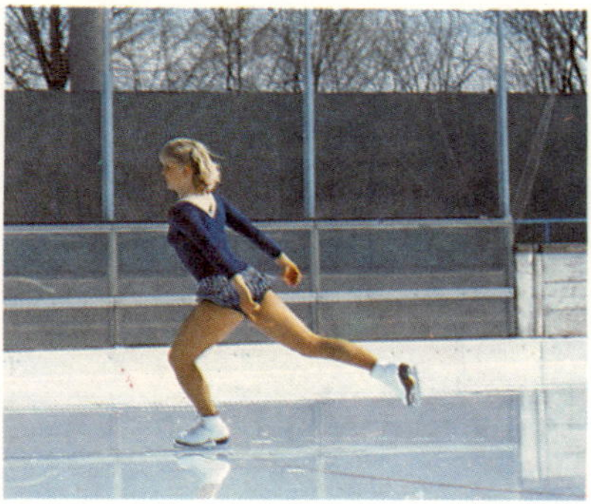
3

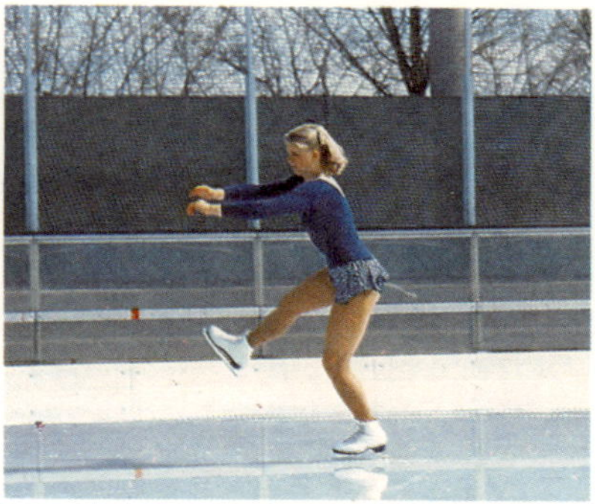
4

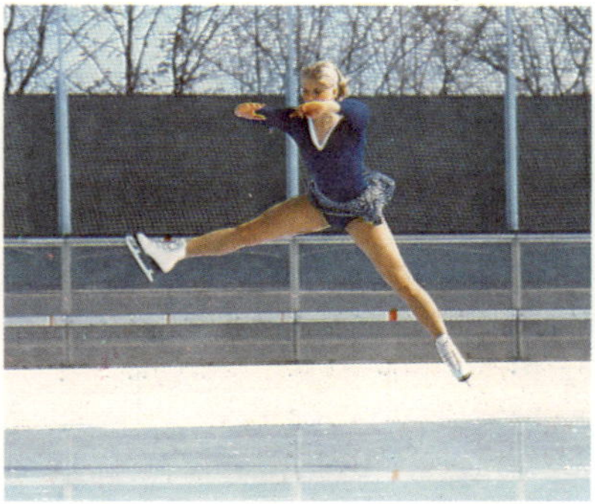
5

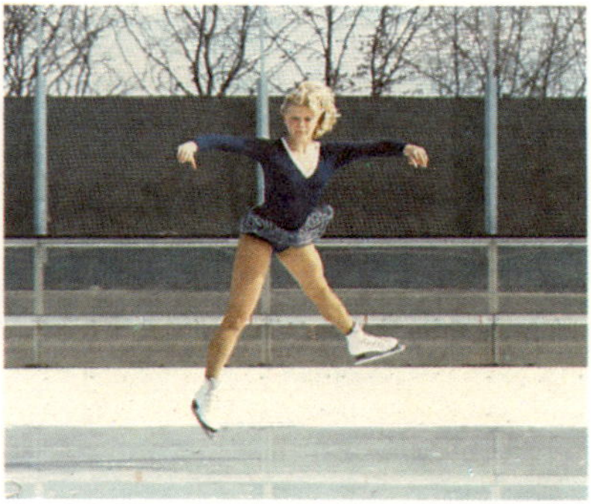
6

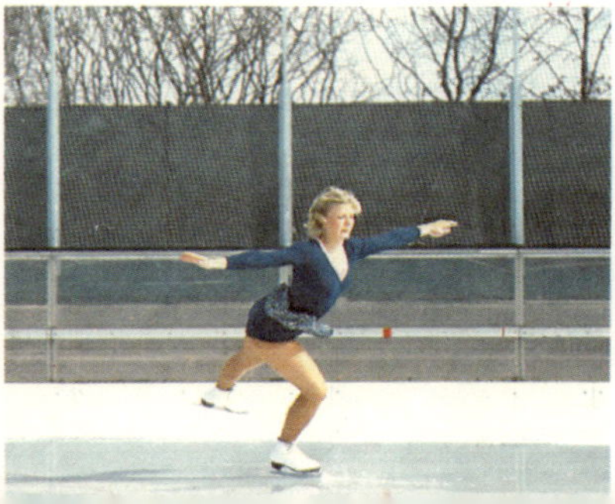
7

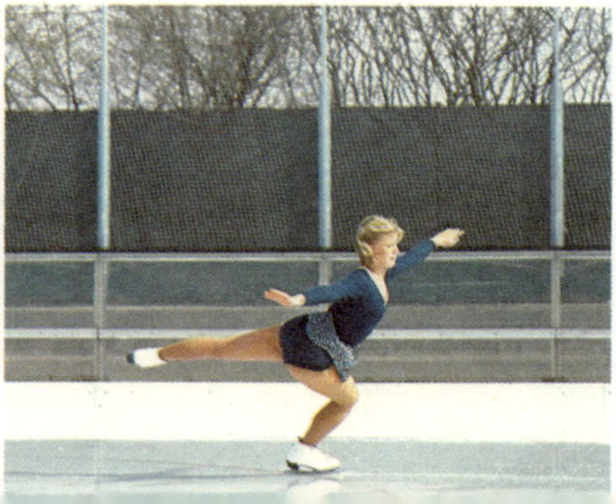
8

Skating school II

Basic principles

There are two main groups here, the two-foot and the one-foot spins. Once again there are so many variations of the latter that they cannot all be listed since there are simply no limits to one's imagination.

However the most important features here are always good rotation and the correct speed, ie the revolutions should be centred on one spot, without any so-called 'wandering'.

Like jumps, spins also consist of three equally important phases:
- The approach and start
- The actual turning
- The finishing off

'Wandering', the sign of a badly executed spin.

1. Two-foot spin

Let us begin with the two-foot pirouette, which can be started from a standing position.

Technique

Stand with your legs slightly apart and forward in the direction of travel. To achieve the necessary momentum, bend both knees at the same time, moving your left arm to the front and your right arm back, but both to the right. You should then be looking over your right shoulder. If you straighten up again now, again bring your arms to the front at the same moment and pull them close into your body, keeping them rounded. You should then be facing straight ahead again.

Tips

- It is important not to have your chin tucked in. You must look straight ahead on to the ice to prevent any feeling of giddiness.
- Your centre of gravity must always be in the middle of your rotating skates.
- The shorter (but not jerkier) your arm and shoulder movements turn out to be, co-ordinated with the high-low movements of your legs, the more revolutions you will make on the ice.

Mistakes

Both skates are on the ice. If you come forward in to your toe rakes, your speed is reduced and no more revolutions will be possible. You will lose your

Spins

balance and have to save yourself from falling or stumbling by quickly changing your leg positions.

If rotation slows down at the end, put your weight on your right leg and stretch your left leg out behind you. Open your arms, with the left one in front and the right one behind, so that you are in a counter-position with your skating leg bent. You should be looking over your right shoulder into the circle.

Of course there are always skaters who, when spinning, prefer to revolve in the opposite direction.

Summary

Low-high movement of both legs – move both arms to left – straighten up – curve arms in to body – finishing off with counter-position – skating leg on left backward outside – right leg stretched out behind.

1 Start of two-foot spin.
2 Getting momentum from the knee.
3 Loosely close legs and arms.
4 Head faces loosely forward.

Spins

2. One-foot standing spin

Rotate backward inside. You must skate the start of the spin correctly to achieve the right speed and to keep your balance.

Technique
Learn the preparation for this with a short right-hand curve backward inside in the counter-position, with the knee bent. When straightening up, pull up your free foot which was stretched out behind and bring it down forward outside to start the Three immediately. Give your left arm as powerful a swing as possible from the shoulder backwards, then move it at shoulder height to the upper part of the body together with the right arm. Hold your forearms there bent and pressed together. When the spin loses momentum, open your arms out again.

While you are rotating in the Three with your knee bent, move your free right foot just above the ice to trace a wide curve. Then put out your free foot high up at right angles to your torso and move it to the front. At this point

1   *Preparation RBI.*
2   *Start LFO.*
3   *Free leg moves gently over ice.*
4-7 *Move bent free leg from behind to front in wide arc.*
8-9 *Bring down leg RBO and finish off.*

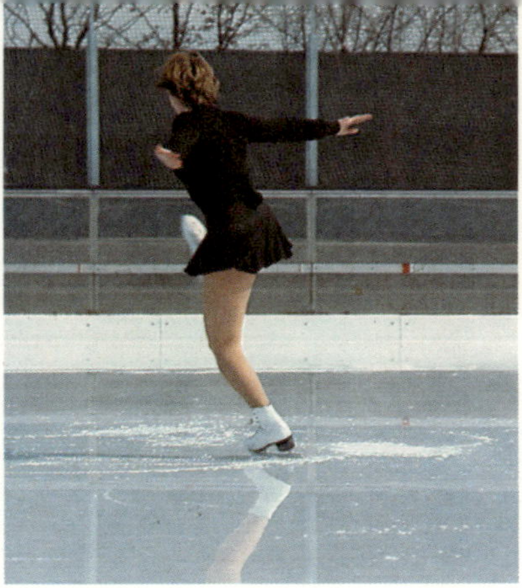
4

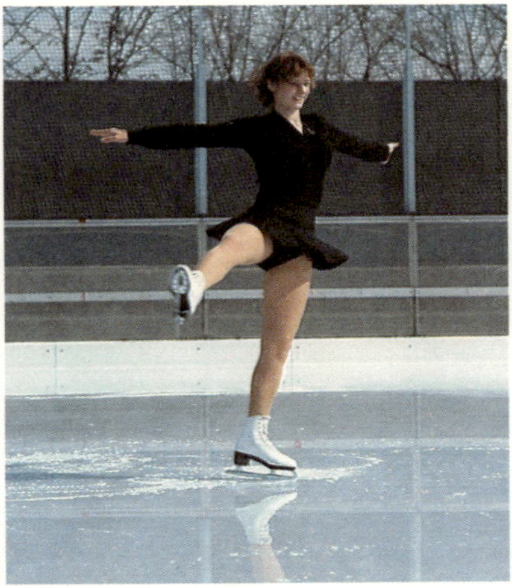
5

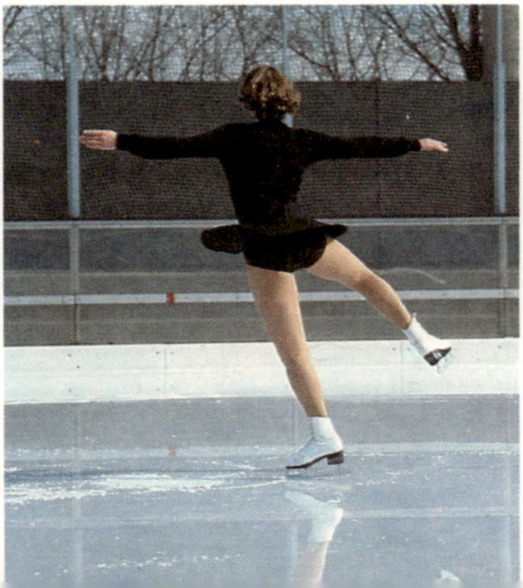
6

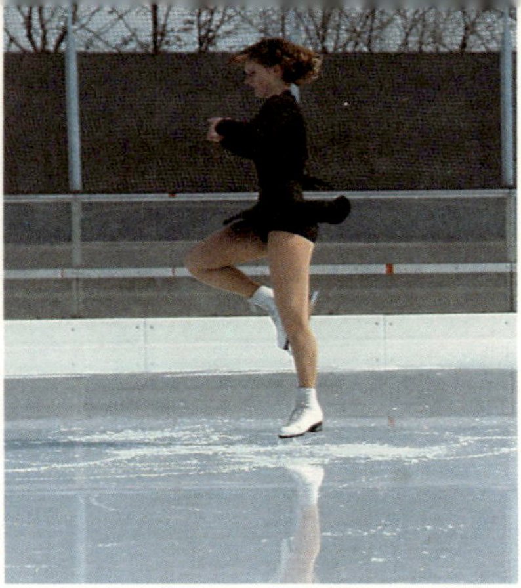
7

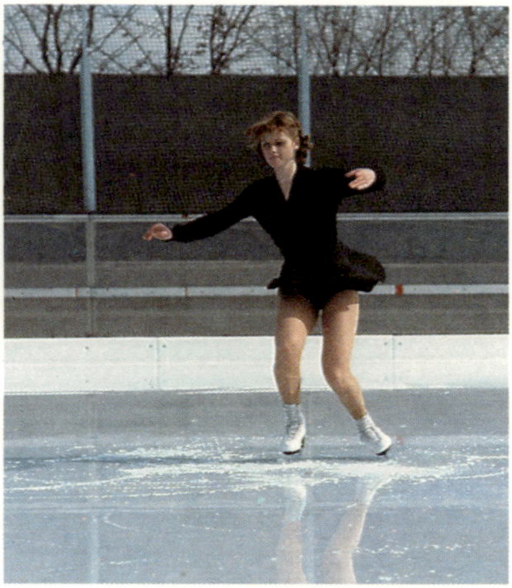
8

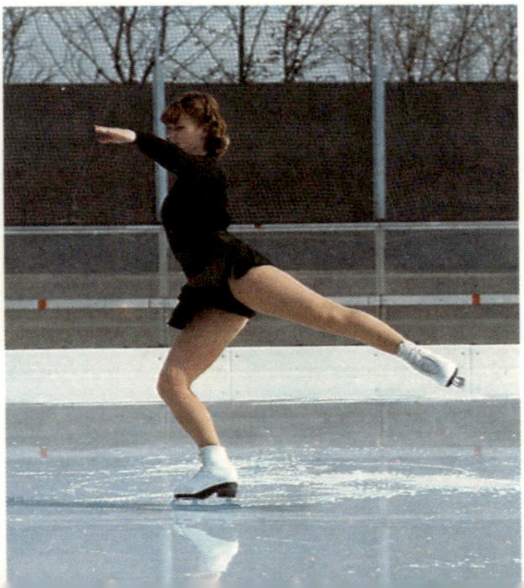
9

Skating school II

bend your lower leg so that the toe of your free leg, which is pointing downwards, is held approximately at the height of your skating knee.

Important
- As you revolve, take care not to let the toe rakes dig into the ice since this would slow you down and possibly cause loss of balance, with the chance of a fall.
- The centre of gravity for your body – as in the two-foot spin – must be in the middle of your rotating skates. Thus the whole of your body must be an upright position. This means that your head is free and straight, your chin is not tucked in and your head is not under any circumstances twisted over your inner or outer shoulder. Otherwise your body would no longer form an axis and a centred spin would be impossible.
- Before the last rotating momentum is over, slowly move your free right leg close up to your skating leg and down to the ice, putting it down with your knee bent backward outside. At the same time open out your arms so that you make a backward outside curve as a finish in the counter-position. Here your head should move with the rest of your body.

Summary
for the opposite direction

Preparation left backward inside in counter-position – immediate start of Three from right forward outside to backward inside – swing right arm back as far as possible – then bring it up to upper part of body – move free left foot just above ice – make wide curve from behind to front – bend – face straight ahead – finish on left backward outside – counter-position.

3. Sit spin

When you can do the one-foot standing spin without difficulty, try the sit spin backward inside. The entire preparation and start is as in the standing spin. Only, after kicking your free leg forward, do not stretch your skating leg any more but bend the whole of your torso into your knee. Your goal should then be to squat down so far that you can almost sit on the heel of your skating foot's blade.

1   *Start LFO.*
2 & 3   *Free leg swings forward in a wide arc over the ice.*
4   *Skating leg bent in squatting position.*
5   *Thighs together.*
6   *Pull up using your back.*

Spins

Skating school II

Important
- The body's centre of gravity plays a particularly important part in the sit spin. When beginning, you still stick your toe rakes gently into the ice. But then by shifting your weight further back you will quickly achieve success.
- Take care that you not only want to get sitting low down, but that you let yourself be supervised and corrected when going into a sitting position. When you are rotating you can completely lose your feeling of depth in the sitting position.

Preliminary practice
Try the 'pistol' for preliminary practice; this is a simple, but extremely strenuous, exercise. Skate forward and then stretch one leg out in front. It is best to keep your arms at shoulder height in front of you. Now try to go down into a sitting position in which your free leg should be held stretched out in front of you. Bend the upper part of your body forward to the thigh of your skating leg, keeping your legs close together. Initially you can only go down into a sitting position with both legs and then stretch out one leg in front for the 'pistol'. If you are fit, try to stand up again.

To do this, first pull yourself up by your back, pressing your arms firmly down – and your free leg, too. When you have reasonably grasped the 'pistol', the sitting position in the sit spin should no longer be any problem.

Technique
While you are bending down to your skating foot you should keep your free leg, which has come forward, in front. But now hold it slightly bent in front of your skating foot, keeping your thighs well together. Your elongated back and the skate on your skating foot should form a line. In the sitting position, bend your arms in front at shoulder height and lay one on top of the other. Coming up is difficult, but do so as in the 'pistol'. Pull yourself up by first using your back, initially pressing your free leg down as a counter weight. Press your arms down too to ease the strain on your back further. Only when you are standing with your skating leg almost straight should you bring up your free leg as well – and afterwards set it down on the ice. Finish off again with a backward

Spins

outside curve in the counter-position.

Everything mentioned above applies in the same context to the sit spin on your skating right leg. Carry out the preparation and start, as well as the finish, exactly as for the standing spin on the right leg.

Balance spin

4. Balance spin

If you enjoy spins, you should now try the backward inside balance spin.

As a preliminary to this, make a right backward inside curve with the knee well bent in the counter-position.

Technique
When straightening up, pull in your free foot (which was stretched out behind) and put it down forward outside as an immediate start to the Three. Swing your left arm as far back as possible from the shoulder and immediately afterwards move it forwards, keeping it straight and at shoulder height. Keep your right arm behind at the same height. Face forward, a little towards your left shoulder.

Important
- Look straight ahead without glancing at the ice. You must feel a heavy strain on your shoulder blades as you did in the camel in **Skating School I**. While your right arm is pulled back, your left arm must be held firmly forward for the counter-pull.
- When you have moved your arms into this position, your skating leg will meanwhile have carried out the Three to left backward inside and your knee should now be markedly bent. Bend your torso forward and parallel to the ice until it is positioned exactly over your left thigh. Keep your free right leg behind you and just above the ice during the Three. Then pull it up high from behind and stretch it out horizontally, thus forming a line with the upper part of your body.
- Take care that you pull your right arm back; but the shoulder itself should point as far as possible forward and parallel to the ice. This has less to do with the correctness of the balance figure than with the rotation itself.

Skating school II

- If your right shoulder is also pulled back, there is a risk that your whole torso will twist backwards in the same way and there will be no more tension in your body. You will find that rotation in the balance position then becomes impossible since your body's centre of gravity is no longer over the rotating skate on your skating leg. The circles get bigger, which unavoidably results in your coming out of the spin.
- When the momentum of the spin slows down, gradually straighten up the upper part of your body and bring your free leg down to your skating leg. Then move your arms to your body, slightly bent at hip height. When you bring your right skate down on to the ice backward outside, open them out again so that your left arm moves forward and your right arm goes back; lower the shoulder so that you can look over it.

Summary
for the opposite direction:

Preparation left backward inside – immediate start of Three right forward outside to backward inside – swing your right arm far out behind and afterwards move it back forward – face straight ahead – upper part of body parallel to ice – raise left leg behind until horizontal – when rotation slows, straighten up upper part of body – move free leg to skating foot – bring it down left backward outside – open arms – finish in counter-position.

5. Spin combinations

There are really no limits to the imagination. On television or in ice shows you will see an enormous number of variations with leg changes, jumping in, jumping round etc. We will concentrate here on the simpler changes in body and leg positions. After the one-foot standing spin, you can try out straight away further spinning on both feet, which is easy to do, and also rotating in a standing spin after a sitting spin. However, a combination of balance and sitting spins does above all require good technique and correct mastery of the different elements. It is enjoyable to watch the contrast of the stretched body position in the balance and the 'folded-up' sit spin in the sitting position, which comes over very effectively. Each element of the spin should consist of at least three revolutions.

Spins

Technique
After three rotations in the balance, gently bring your front arm to the side and then swing it back straight away with the back arm and bring it to the upper part of your body; but make sure it is bent.

In so doing, bring your free leg, which was stretched out behind, to the front in a wide arc (as in the start to the sit spin). While you are changing the position of your arms and legs, straighten up your torso again and go down on your skating leg into a deep sitting position to rotate in a sit spin. Then finish again as in the previous one-foot spins.

Change from the balance to the sit spin.

Skating school II – Curve skating

You are already familiar with the basic forms of the compulsory figures from the starts and preliminaries of jumps and spins. However, to be able to perform the steps, jumps and turns more cleanly and correctly, you must learn the basic concepts of curve-skating. Only then can you improve your performance in free skating.

In the simple curve eights skated forwards and backwards on both legs symmetrically, you generally begin on your right leg. Skate each figure three times on each leg.

Tips
- For compulsory skating you are recommended to look for a part of the ice that has been as little used as possible. The track of your skate should still be visible after completion of the compulsory figure. Above all, this makes it easier to find the starting point, ie the beginning, again.
- Initially, as an aid, use a bit of ice scraped with the blade as a marker for the start.
- Now let us construct the figure. Your start mark should lie roughly in the middle of the area. The surface available should be twice the size of your body on all four sides. That is enough to start with. At the start itself, have your arms in an open position and your legs closed. Only take up the required body position for the take-off.

1. Curve eight forward outside

Technique
Stand in the closed position at the start mark, turn your torso and head to the right, lowering your right shoulder. Hold your right arm in front and loosely at hip height, while pointing your left arm behind. Turn out your right foot and put it down at right angles to the left skating foot at the instep, with the knees well bent. Now, shifting your whole body weight on to your skating leg, take off powerfully using your right foot.

Important
- Under no circumstances should your toe rakes stick into the ice when taking off. You must take off using the whole skate blade. After the shift of weight on to the right leg, the free leg (now the left one) should remain behind with the foot turned out, but otherwise loosely stretched.
- To trace the shape of the circle on the ice, press your right shoulder, which is inside, deep and quite markedly into the circle. But you must keep your right arm in front to form a line

Take-off for the curve eight forward outside.

Shift of weight to forward outside.

with your right skate, as otherwise you could unwittingly rotate into a Three.
- When skating in a circle, in fact, and not just an endless curve, you will find a large part is played by the rhythmical sequence of movements of your arm and leg positions.
- If you divide the figure into three imaginary parts, you have learned the first third with the take-off and balancing. Now slowly bring your free leg up close and parallel to your skating leg, past it and to the front. In the last third of the curve, also move your left arm to the front; your right arm, however, goes behind you. At the end of the circle, pull your free leg from the front up to your free right leg to regain the starting point with your skates parallel to one another. Just before the marker point, take your right skating foot out of the track and move it gently into the circle you have just skated. In this way you will achieve a better take-off for your free left foot.

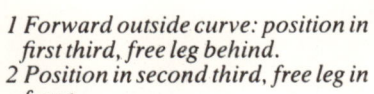

1 Forward outside curve: position in first third, free leg behind.
2 Position in second third, free leg in front.
3 Curve eight forward inside: start position.
4 Take-off.
5 Shifting weight to FI.

Curve skating

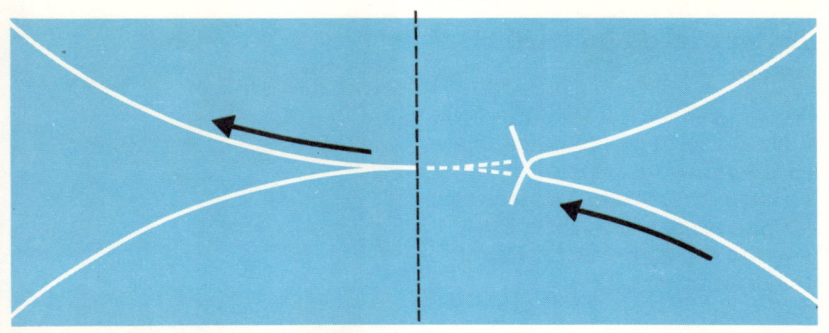

Diagram of foot changes in a curve eight FO.

Technique

Put your left foot exactly on the starter mark, with your knee well bent, and give a powerful push-off. The skating foot helps in the push-off, but without the toe rakes becoming embedded in the ice. Your left arm should now be in front with your left shoulder lower down and pointing into the circle. Look towards the track to be skated. During the first third, your right arm is behind. Slowly straighten up from the knee, then bring your out-turned free leg, which was loosely stretched out behind, slowly up to your skating foot, past it and to the front. In the last third of the curve, bring your arms smoothly into the open position until you reach the starter mark. Bring your left skate gently into the circle you have just finished, once more to be in the right position for taking off again with the right foot.

Of course you will have difficulty in your first attempts to find your track again or even to skate in it. You will probably find that your circle has become 'egg-shaped'. But at the beginning this is quite natural. It is not that easy to correct the 'egg' shape and make a circle-like pattern after just a few attempts.

A large part is also played by ice conditions, the prevailing wind at the time, general weather and, of course, your take-off or momentum. You must first learn to give the correct value to the sequence of movements, to change and to carry them out. Altogether this means a lot of hard work requiring lots of time and stamina.

Skating school II

2. Curve eight forward inside

Your curve track from the outside eight is almost certainly no longer recognizable – or at least scratched too much. Turn round 90° and make a new track. But you can still make further use of the old starter mark.

Technique
Again stand in the open position with your legs closed and twist the upper part of your body and your head to the right. Then take up a counter-position for the take-off; this means: left arm in front, left shoulder lowered into the circle and face towards the track to be skated.

Move your right arm back.
For the start, take your weight on your left leg and bring your right leg down on to the ice, turned slightly inside, with the

Counter-position in first third.

knee bent and pushing off strongly. Position your left skate to help in this but do not let the toe rakes bite into the ice under any circumstances. Stretch your left leg (now the free one) losely out behind, keeping the toe turned out. Slowly straighten up

Diagram of foot changes in a curve eight forward inside.

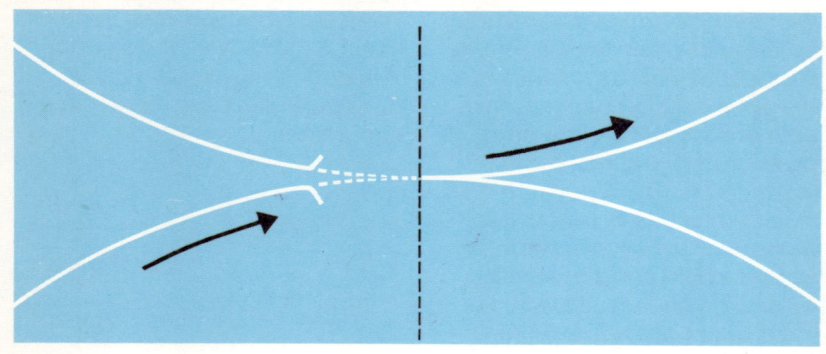

Curve skating

Position in second third, free leg in front.

Position in last third: arm changes.

from the knee, having then almost mastered the first third of the circle. While you lean your left arm markedly into the circle, slowly pull your free leg closely past your skating foot and to the front, keeping it just in front of your skating foot. Your knees should be pressed closely together, making it easier to keep your balance. Finish skating your inside curve with your legs in this position. Slowly move your right arm forward and bring the left one back. Just before the marker point, shift the weight on your skating leg briefly from the inside to the outside edge and virtually skate out of the circle into the new one to be skated left forward inside.

Put your left foot, with the knee bent, inside on the ice at the instep of your right skate, pushing off powerfully from the ice. You can get your right foot to help with the start by keeping its entire blade on the ice without the toe rakes becoming embedded into the ice. As you straighten up slowly, keep your free leg loosely stretched out behind with the toe turned out in the track of your skating leg. Lean your right arm far into the centre of the circle. Slowly move your free leg closely up to your skating foot, past it and slightly in front. While doing this, press your knees closely together again.

Skating school II

Important
- While your free leg is moving, lean your torso very slightly backwards – or, to put it better, push your pelvis and hips forward. This helps you keep your balance. Finish skating the inside curve with your body in this position. Slowly move your left arm in front, changing your right arm to behind you.
- Just before the marker point, briefly shift the weight of your skating leg from the inside edge to the outside edge and once more skate the circle previously skated on your right leg. During this brief change of edge (only really skating ahead), bring your free leg up and then down on the ice at your left instep; make sure it is turned slightly inwards and the knee is bent. But do not let the toe rakes bite into the ice. This way you will ensure a powerful push-off.
- By moving out into the new curve and briefly changing edge, which is really only skating straight ahead, you will get into a good starting position for your new skating leg.
- It is important not to make a 'step' when changing, but put

Diagram showing the correct point for the change from LFO to RFO with characteristic long and short axis.

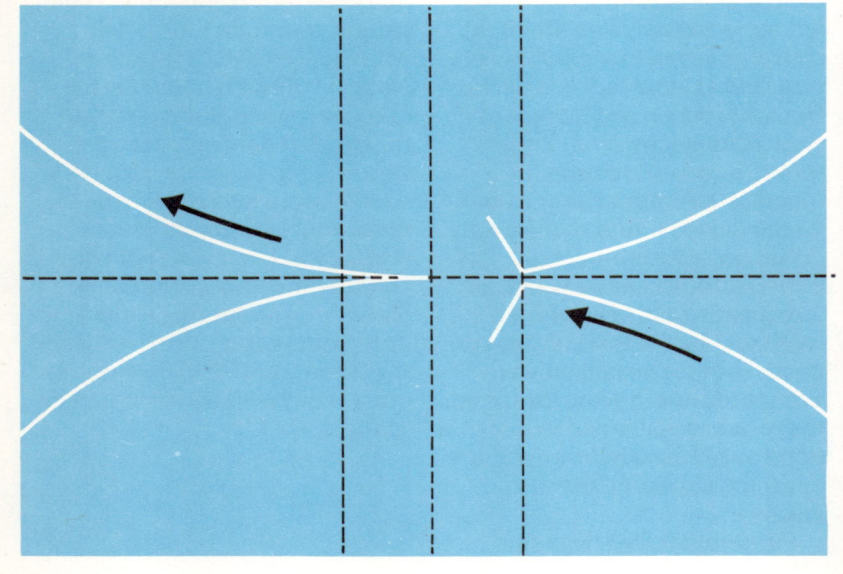

Curve skating

your new skating leg down almost closed at the instep of your previous skating leg. Only this way can you bring your whole body under control, thereby keeping your balance.
- When first practising, you will see how the curve can be divided into three clear parts. Those who do not arrive back where the starter point is visible are either skating their curves too large or are taking their weight on the appropriate edge so that it falls into the circle (the same in outside and inside curves) and then bringing in the free leg to help.
- With the first few attempts it is perhaps easier if, right at the beginning of the compulsory skating, you bring small markers to pick out the curve to be skated. A glove, skate guard, small pile of snow etc would be enough.
- But, above all, you should mark the difficult points where the positions of your arms or legs change. Very gradually a rhythm will, of its own accord, come into this sequence of movements and in time you will be skating recognizable curves that no longer have anything in common with 'eggs'.
- The ideal curve area is a circle three times the height of the skater. But this criterion is only valid in championships and competitions. At the beginning you must always bear in mind that it is difficult to manage a powerful push-off.
- When your momentum slackens and you begin to wobble, ie you change uncertainly from one edge to the other on your skating foot, you should give a quick – but powerful – kick with your free leg and then finish the curve.

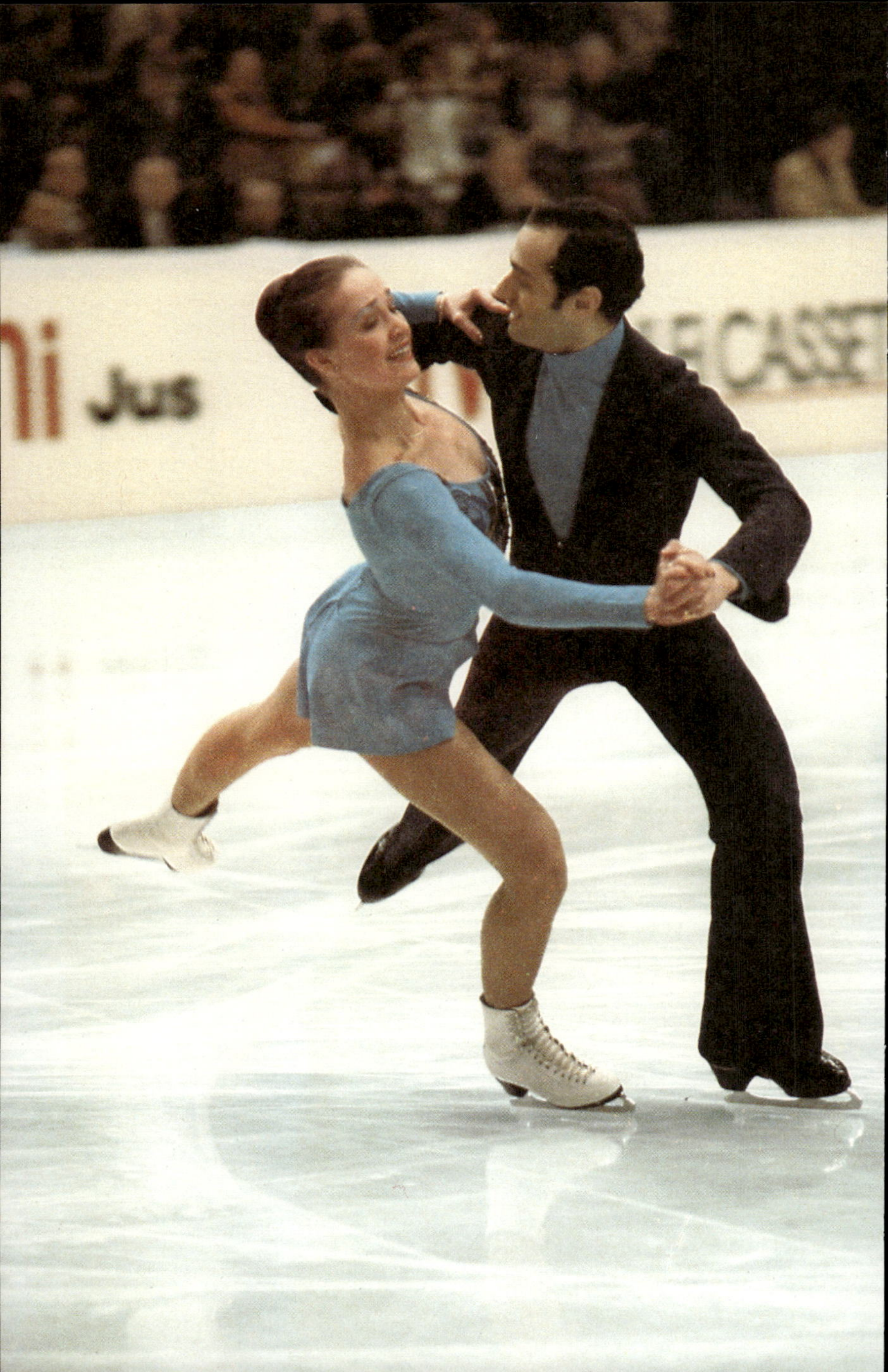
Jus

Ice dancing

If you are happy not to have to continue any further with compulsory skating and do not want to conjure up any more acrobatic jumps and spins on the ice, you will certainly find pleasure in the gliding movements of ice dancing.

Although there are at least 18 compulsory dances for competitions and dancing tests that have to be skated with a precisely described or preferred diagram and a sequence of steps which you must adhere to exactly, we shall firstly concentrate on a relatively simple waltz. Later you can use steps from **Skating School I**, which are supplemented by special dance steps.

1. Dance holds

At the outset, here is a brief explanation of the different holds which were extensively taken over from social dancing.

Hand-in-hand hold
Choose the hand-in-hand hold to start with: the woman stands on the man's right and holds the man's outstretched right hand with her hand also outstretched at a comfortable distance. Both partners face in the same direction.

Hand-in-hand hold to start with.

Ice dancing

Waltz hold
In the closed or waltz hold the partners stand exactly opposite one another with shoulders parallel. One skates forwards and the other backwards. The woman's left hand lies on the man's right shoulder. The man's left arm and the woman's right arm are kept loosely stretched out at shoulder height, while the man's right hand almost rests on the woman's shoulder blade.

Kilian hold
The Kilian hold is important. Both partners look in the same direction, with the woman always standing on the right. Her left arm is held stretched out in front of the man and she holds his left hand. The man holds his right arm outstretched behind the woman's back, holding her waist with his right hand. As far as possible you should skate hip-to-hip, which is particularly difficult to do.

Dance holds

Tips
- Since all of the ice-dancing steps have to be practised alone at first, every singles skater can also do ice dancing, although you do not necessarily have to join up as a pair with someone else later.
- Since each dance is skated to a certain rhythm and you must therefore pay attention to the beat and tempo of the music, counting to a certain rhythm makes skating much easier and initially replaces music.
- The Chassé, double-time step and change step, which we have already practised in **Skating School I**, also occur in almost every dance. The cross steps to be skated forward and backwards crossed either in front or behind, which were likewise mentioned in detail in the section on **Steps**, also belong to these.

Foxtrot hold
For many dances the open or foxtrot hold is also required. (The outer or tango hold is not included in this section.) The foxtrot hold is included in the foxtrot and rocker foxtrot; it also occurs in other compulsory dances combined with other dance holds.

Ice dancing

The dancing Three hold.

2. Dancing Three

There is only a slight difference between this and the normal Three step. You skate the dancing Three using the closed or waltz hold. The difficulty lies less in the Three itself than in the position of the shoulders, which must be absolutely parallel.

During the Three and subsequent steps, the skaters must stand close to one another face-to-face so that the partner who is turning is not 'flung', ie falls out of the circle. With this close hold precise footwork is very important too. You skate the dancing Three in a counter-clockwise direction, which means on the left leg. For some dances, however, you can also skate it in the opposite direction, but we shall not go into that at the moment.

Technique
Start the dancing Three with the knee well bent in towards the middle of the circle. As you straighten up, bring your free right leg from behind up parallel to your skating leg and hold it just above the ice. During the Three itself your legs remain straight. Immediately after the turn, place your right leg with the knee bent down on to the ice. Bring your free left leg forward with your toe turned out again just above the ice.

Beating time for the Three
- In this Three, it is advisable to count time to get the rhythm of this typical waltz step. Make the Three turn itself on **Three**, which means:
- **One** = bring down leg with knee bent.
- **Two** = straighten up with skating leg and bring up free leg close to it.
- **Three** is then the turn backward.
- **Four** = bring down previous free leg with knee bent.
- **Five** = straighten up with skating leg and
- **Six** = pull up your free leg again to closed position.

Then start off again with **One** = bring down leg forward outside with bent knee in front.

1 Beginning of the woman's Three.

2 Turn is made exactly in front of the man.

3 Partners with feet in closed position.

4 Woman turns backward, man forward.

Ice dancing

It is important to make the three turn on **Three**. This sequence of movements gives elegance and a flowing rhythm to the steps.

Important
- Counting is indispensable when skating the dancing Three with a partner. Then your partner starts the Three on **Four**, but starts counting for himself/herself at **One**. Therefore when the woman has turned from forward outside to backward inside and has placed her right foot backward outside on to the ice, her partner starts on the left forward outside with the knee bent, straightens up and turns his Three to backward inside (= **Three**). And while he is bringing down his right foot backward outside, the woman begins again with the start of another Three.
- This sequence of Threes can be skated over all the available ice surface. When you get these sequences of movements flowing, you can also skate the Three movements in a figure of eight. In principle you then perform the same movements, but change direction at the middle of the ice rink and therefore the direction of your Three turn.

Technique
The woman brings down her right leg forward outside with the knee well bent (**One**), straightens up the skating leg and brings up the free leg to the closed position (**Two**) and then turns the Three to right backward inside (on **Three**). When the woman brings down the left foot with the knee well bent backward inside (**Four**), her partner starts his Three once again – with **One** (the knee well bent right forward outside).

In both directions of the turn, both skaters must take care that they face one another (using the closed or waltz hold) and do not change to the open or tango hold (hip-to-hip). Then one partner would have to 'skate round' the other during the turn.

3. Mohawk

This dance step has many uses and can be skated in many variations – for instance open, closed, inside and outside. For the Fourteen you need the open Mohawk. The man uses the inside Mohawk and the woman the outside Mohawk; and we will start with the latter.

Mohawk

Outside Mohawk

Technique

After the preliminary movements counter-clockwise, begin the open Mohawk with your knee bent left forward outside and straighten up with your body in the open position. Look towards the barrier with your back to the middle of the circle. Pull up your free right leg and put your heel on to the ice backward outside at the instep of your skating foot and in its track. Immediately stretch out your left leg (now the free one) behind briefly, with the toe turned out, then move it back to your skating foot and bring it down closed backward inside.

Important

- The foot change is accordingly made from the outside edge once more to the outside edge; in the open Mohawk the curve shape is equally pronounced both at the beginning and the end of the curve.
- The last starting step of the man's steps is skated left forward outside.

Inside Mohawk

Technique

Start the Mohawk with the knee bent right forward inside. As you straighten up, pull up your free left leg from behind, putting it down on the ice with your heel at the instep of your right skate in its track backward inside. During this direction change, you should have your back to the barrier. Face into the middle of the circle. The next step will then be right backward outside.

Important

This time the foot change is made from the inside edge to the inside edge again. The shape of the curve at the beginning and end of the Mohawk again remains equally pronounced.

Open Mohawk from FO to BO.

Open Mohawk from FI to BI.

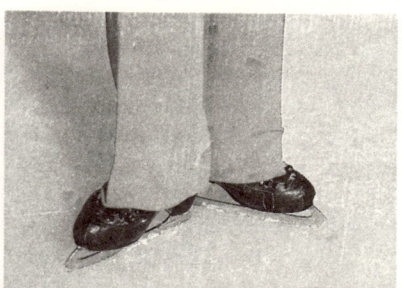

Ice dancing

Open Choctaw from forward inside to backward outside.

4. Choctaw

We will finish off the preparation for our first dances with the open Choctaw, which we need for the Kilian. This Choctaw is an ideal step too as it can equally be skated open, closed, from outside to inside or the other way round.

You dance your open Choctaw from forward inside to backward outside. To make proper preparation for the Kilian, arrange for it to be added later in the dance. Both skaters do the Choctaw at the same time.

Technique

The starting position is forward counter-clockwise. For this, stand right outside and bring your free left leg up from behind, crossing it over to the outside edge of your skating foot. With your knee well bent, put your left foot down forward inside and skate an exaggerated inside curve. Hold your free foot in front slightly above the ice. As you straighten up slowly, move your free right foot to the inside edge of your skating foot and place it on the ice at this point backward outside, with the knee slightly bent. After this shift of weight, keep your free left leg close behind your skating right foot, bringing it down backward inside again with the knee bent.

Face the barrier during this series of steps, your back towards the inside of the circle.

1   *Beginning forward inside with knee bent.*
2 & 3 *Free leg close to skating foot; straighten up with shoulders back to backward outside.*
4   *Finishing off.*

Choctaw

Dances

Basic principles

In all the steps used in preparation for the following dances, a little extra is required for dancing. In ice dancing, as in social dancing, the character of a dance is expressed in its movements. In the first place you must pay attention to rhythm, which marks out the music's expression and individuality. This means a group of notes, which can be as long as you like. The notes can be emphasized or not, as well as long or short, and can be repeated constantly. In addition there is tempo, which means the speed of the music into which the number of strokes of the ice are divided according to the beat.

Counting the length of the step to be skated is therefore important. For example, in a dance Three of **One** to **Six**. **One** and **Two** = beginning, **Three** = Three turn, **Four** = bringing down free leg and **Five** and **Six** = finishing off with the free leg. Since the strokes of the ice not only determine the beat of the dance Three, but also the open Mohawk and the open Choctaw, as well as the change step etc, and convey its character and rhythm, the strokes are also given in the diagram sketches for the dances that follow.

1. Glide waltz

This circular dance is no longer required in competitive skating, but it is a help when you are first concerned with counting. In this way, moreover, you can to start with do without music. You can bring out the rhythm of a dance just as well by continuous counting. In this case a slow waltz is also known as an English waltz. The glide waltz is skated in the Kilian hold. Skate four preliminary forward strokes to give yourself momentum for the glide. Start at the corner of the ice rink, with each partner only holding each other's hands. The lady stands on the right holding her partner's right hand. The first step is left forward outside,

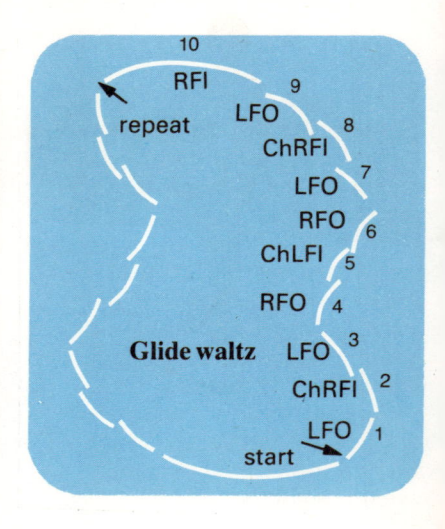

```
           10
        RFI      9
repeat     LFO     8
              ChRFI
              LFO    7
              RFO    6
              ChLFI  5
              RFO    4
 Glide waltz  LFO    3
              ChRFI  2
              LFO    1
           start
```

Glide waltz

followed by right, left, right. After the first two steps the partners use the Kilian hold and on reaching the long axis they begin with the first sequence of steps:

Men's and women's steps

1 = LFO	beat 1
2 = Chassé RFI	1
3 = LFO	2
4 = RFO	1
5 = Chassé LFI	1
6 = RFO	2
7 = LFO	1
8 = Chassé RFI	1
9 = LFO	2
10 = long curve RFI	4

Technique
Skate a Chassé left, right, left towards the middle of the rink. At the same time count: **One** = left forward outside, **Two** = briefly put right foot down close to skating left foot and **Three** and **Four** = hold the step for longer left forward outside and straighten up from the knee in an exaggerated manner.

Afterwards do a Chassé towards the barrier, therefore starting from forward outside with the right foot (= **One**).

Long drawn-out curve FI in the glide waltz.

Two is again bringing down your foot briefly, but this time on the left next to your right skating foot. For **Three** and **Four** hold the step for longer right forward outside and straighten up from the knee in an exaggerated manner.

Then do another Chassé to the middle of the rink left, right, left in four beats, too = **One**, **Two** and **Three**, **Four**.

If you have followed the diagram described above for the dance, ie the sketch of the tracks, you should now have reached the short axis of the rink again and there you should start a long, drawn-out, only slightly rounded curve right forward inside, which you should hold for a while. For this step, too, count **One, Two, Three, Four**.

Dances

During the long curve, keep your free leg behind you. Straighten up your skating leg very slowly from the knee, but in a flowing movement. At the fourth beat move up your free left leg to begin another Chassé towards the middle of the circle, on reaching the long axis. Now you should have the first step sequence of the glide waltz behind you. In fact, to demonstrate this marked gliding, you have to skate round several times.

Waltz hold until Step 7 of the Fourteen and 'open' hold afterwards.

Important
- The long inside curves should as far as possible be exactly opposite one another and should fill up the short axis of the ice rink. If the ice rink is fairly small, you must skate the outside or inside edges in exaggerated fashion. However, on a large surface the Chassés do not need to reach to the barrier or to the middle of the circle. A feeling for dividing up the available space comes with time, as does gliding with momentum.
- Partners must take special care to skate hip-to-hip. Also keep this hold for the long inside curve. In this step the woman must have her shoulders a little in front of her partner. But both should be looking over their left shoulder into the middle of the rink, while in the Chassés their heads should turn to the appropriate direction of travel.

2. Fourteen

The step sequence for this dance consists of 14 steps = 56 beats to every two strokes of the ice since its rhythm is in march time, ie 4/4 time.

Again use the hand-in-hand hold for the beginning, with the woman standing on the right. This time, however, she should perform after the first two preliminary steps to the left on the right leg, a three from left forward outside to left backward inside, skating the three in two strokes. At the same time the man skates two more preliminary steps left, right.

Fourteen

After the woman's Three turn, you should take up the waltz hold in which the partners stand opposite one another. Keep the shoulders parallel. Use this hold up to Step 7. Then, during the woman's or man's turn, take up an open hold until you can start the new sequence of steps with the closed waltz hold.

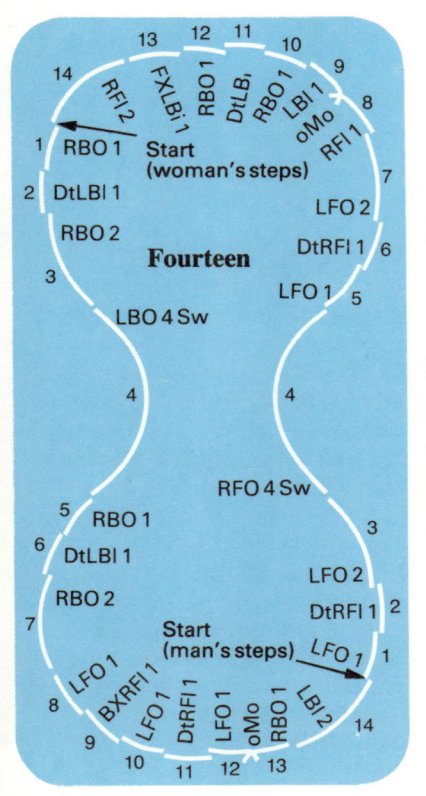

Women's steps

1 = RBO	beats 1
2 = double-time step LBI	1
3 = RBO	2
4 = swing curve LBO	4
5 = RBO	1
6 = double-time step LBI	1
7 = RBO	2
8 = LFO	1
9 = crossed behind RFI	1
10 = LFO	1
11 = double-time step RFI	1
12 = LFO ⎫ open Mohawk	1
13 = RBO ⎭	1
14 = LBI	2

Men's steps

1 = LFO	beats 1
2 = double-time step RFI	1
3 = LFO	2
4 = swing curve RFO	4
5 = LFO	1
6 = double-time step RFI	1
7 = LFO	2
8 = RFI ⎫ open Mohawk	1
9 = LBI ⎭	1
10 = RBO	1
11 = double-time step LBI	1
12 = RBO	1
13 = crossed in front LBI	1
14 = RFI	2

Dances

Fourteen women's steps

Technique
After the preliminary Three, the woman should stand left backward inside. Her first dance step now goes right backward outside to the middle of the circle. Link on a double-time step left backward inside and a step right backward outside, which is held a bit longer. Now follow with a swing curve left backward outside, skated sharply on the outside edge towards the barrier, and hold it for four beats. The woman's free leg moves from the front closely past her skating leg and out behind while her skating leg gradually straightens up from the knee. During the swing curve her head follows the movement of the free leg. She should look over her right shoulder towards the barrier. Then link on a right backward outside step slightly curved to the short axis, followed by a double-time step left backward inside and another step right backward outside, which should be held for longer (two beats). Now with a change in direction to left forward outside the woman enters her step sequence and she should have her back to the middle of the rink. Then she crosses her free right leg closely behind her skating left foot, bringing it down on its outside edge right forward inside.

Swing curve in the Fourteen with the partners' free legs forming a line.

The next step is made left forward outside. Then link on a double-time step right forward inside.

Now follow with an open Mohawk from left forward outside to right backward outside, which you are already familiar with. Link another left backward inside step to it.

Tip
If you consider the previous track diagram and compare it with the sequence of steps skated, you have to be at the opposite long axis of the ice rink, where the next sequence of steps is to start with a right backward outside step towards the middle of the circle.

Fourteen

Fourteen men's steps

It is advisable to practise the step sequences individually at the beginning until you have mastered the timing and the steps. Otherwise you will be put off too easily when your partner has to skate other steps. Take the preliminary steps using the hand-in-hand hold standing on the woman's left, left – right – left – right forward outside.

Technique

For the man, the first step of the Fourteen begins left forward outside towards the middle of the rink. Link on a right double-time step, followed by a left forward outside step, which is held for longer – two beats, in fact.

Then you start the swing curve right forward outside, which must be skated for four strokes sharply on the outside edge. Swing your free leg from behind close up to your skating foot and then out in front, following the movement of the woman's free leg. During this swing curve, which you start with your knee well bent, straighten up slowly. Your head follows the movement of your free leg and faces towards the barrier. Link on a left forward outside step to this, followed by a double-time step right forward inside and another step left forward outside, which again is held for two strokes. Whereas the woman has now changed her direction of travel from backward to forward, the man begins an open Mohawk with a right forward inside step to left backward outside. There follows a right backward outside step, then a double-time step left backward inside and another right backward outside step. Make these three backward steps from the barrier to the short axis in a slight curve. Bring your free left leg up from behind, move it closely past your skating foot and bring it down left backward inside crossed in front of your skating right foot. Move your free leg (now the right one) slightly back and then bring it down right forward inside by changing direction. During the change in direction you should be looking towards the middle of the circle. Carry out this step too, starting with your knee well bent and then straightening up, holding it for two strokes. Now you should have reached the long axis opposite your starting point again and you can now pursue a new step sequence, starting in to the middle of the circle left forward outside.

Dances

3. Kilian

This dance is especially popular since it can be skated with the pair-skating or Kilian hold. But it is nevertheless not without its dangers since it requires a clean-edge technique and precise footwork. The hardest part is skating hip-to-hip and remaining close side-by-side throughout the entire sequence. Since you skate this dance round in a circle, you can start it at any point on the ice. It is useful to start at the short axis with four preliminary steps – left, right, left, right – using the hand-in-hand hold. Take up the Kilian hold during the last step. Start the first dance step roughly in the middle of the short axis.

Although both partners carry out the same sequence of steps, it is useful to practise the passages alone first of all. When you can do the steps cleanly, the partners can attempt to skate them together. Pay particular attention to ensuring your footwork and hold are correct. The Kilian consists of 14 steps as well and is likewise skated in a march rhythm (4/4 or 2/4 time), this time at a speed of 58 beats a minute to every two emphasized strokes.

Technique

After the four preliminary steps, start the Kilian left forward outside, linking it to a right forward inside double-time step, followed by an emphasized step left forward outside, which is held for two strokes. You also skate the next step right forward outside to the barrier for two strokes. Then link on a left forward outside step, a double-time step right forward inside and another step left forward outside.

One problem with the Kilian: the partners must skate hip-to-hip.

Kilian

Now bring up your free right leg from behind, moving it close up to your skating foot and past it. Then bring it down right forward outside, crossing it in front. You have now got to the open Choctaw. Move your free left leg, which is crossed behind, to the outside edge of your skating foot and bring it down forward inside with your knee well bent. Skate an exaggerated inward curve.

Hold your free right foot slightly in front over the ice. This time straighten up quickly, moving your free right leg to the inside edge of your skating foot to bring it down there backward outside, with the knee slightly bent. You should now be standing right backward outside.

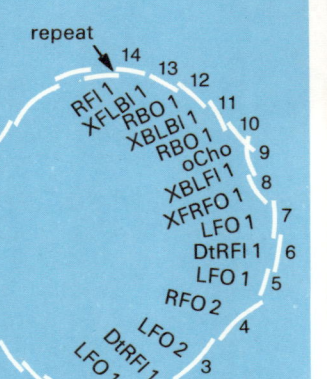

Open Choctaw from FI to BO.

Kilian

repeat
14
13
12
RFI 1
XFLBI 1
RBO 1
XBLBI 1
11
RBO 1
10
oCho
9
XBLFI 1
XFRFO 1 8
LFO 1 7
DtRFI 1 6
LFO 1 5
RFO 2
4
LFO 2
DtRFI 1 3
LFO 1
1 2
start

Men's and women's steps

		beats
1 =	LFO	1
2 =	double-time step RFI	1
3 =	LFO	2
4 =	RFO	2
5 =	LFO	1
6 =	double-time step RFI	1
7 =	LFO	1
8 =	crossed in front RFO	1
9 =	crossed behind LFI } = open Choctaw	1
10 =	RBO	1
11 =	crossed behind LBI	1
12 =	RFO	1
13 =	crossed in front LBI	1
14 =	RFI	1

Dances

1 Starting the Choctaw.
2 Changing from forward inside to backward outside.
3 Finishing off backward outside.

Important
- Take care above all that there is only one stroke available for each step, if you are to keep to the correct rhythm.
- This depends on short, precise steps that are nevertheless clean-edged.
- At the change of direction, stand with your back to the middle of the circle looking towards the barrier. Now bring down your free left foot, which was crossed behind, inside at the outside edge of your right skating foot. Then link on a step right backward outside to that. Bring your left foot down backward inside, crossing it in front of the outside edge of your skating foot. With the upper part of your body and your face towards the middle of the circle, turn on the last step of the Kilian to right forward inside, bringing up your free right foot from behind and setting it down in the track of your left skate.
- Link the new Kilian step sequence to this directly with a left forward outside step, since the fourteenth and last step in this dance only lasts for one beat.

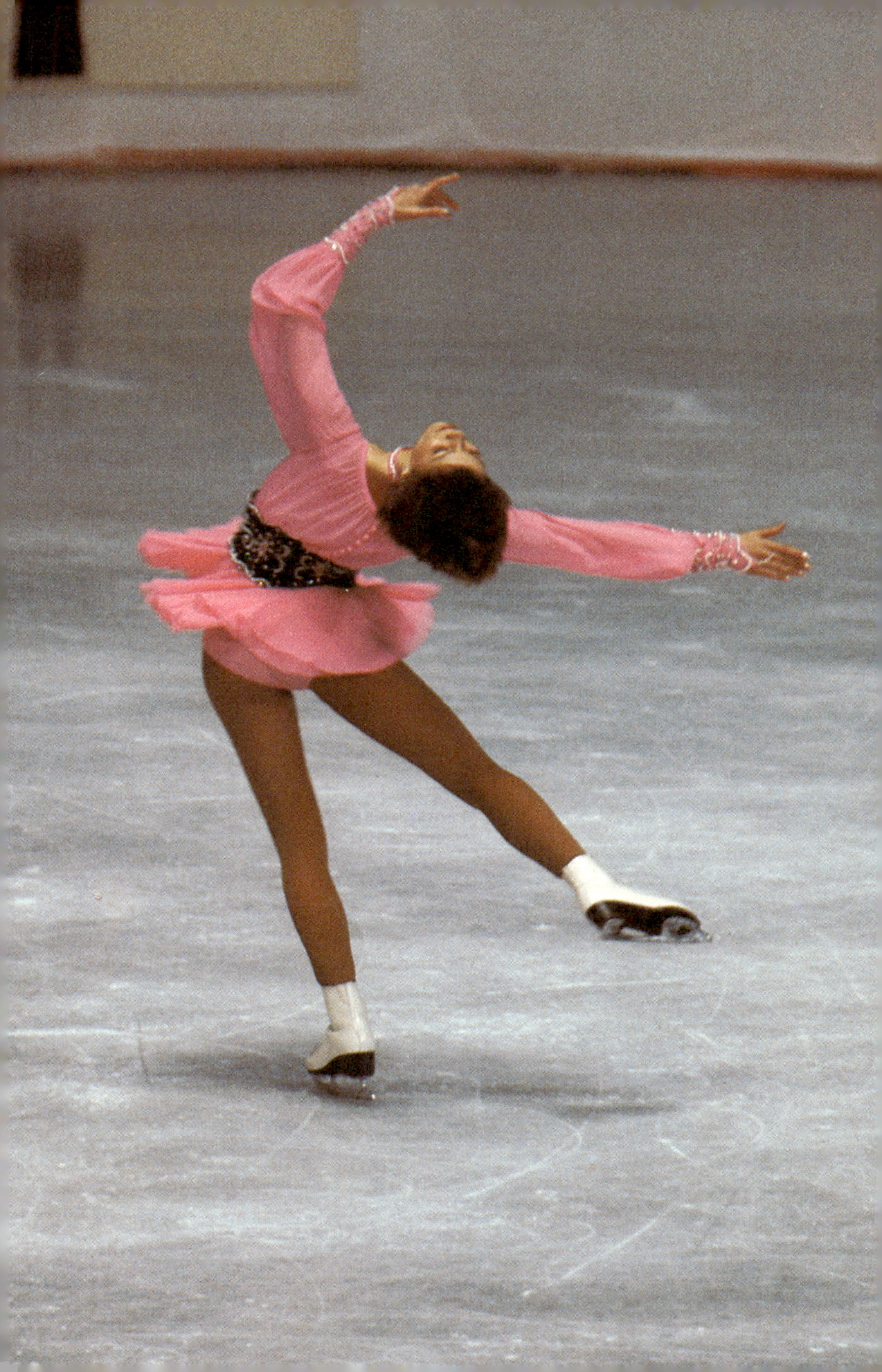

Information on free skating

Denise Bielmann spin. Element of dancing in the performance.

In free skating, you have a choice in putting together the music and in arranging the figures to be executed, which should consist of jumps, spins, combinations of steps and elements of dancing. The skater must express the chosen music in corresponding movements. A free section is built up from free elements, which you can choose yourself, and will be guided by your own ability. Beside championship classes, there are also senior and junior groups. These classes do not reflect the skater's age.

Building up a free programme

In order to get through a free section, which lasts four minutes for women and five minutes for men, skilful arrangement is necessary which can only be worked out after years of training and demands a great variety of ideas.

Generally the free section is divided into three: this includes a dynamic beginning, with difficult elements, for the prelude; then a slower middle section with elements of dancing skilfully woven in and difficult passages that should underline the musical interpretation. The chosen music should correspond to the performer's level of skating. In this second part the skaters

Building up a free programme

should express their personality through their own particular style. In the third part you must still have some reserves of strength for a few difficult sections, which should make up the high point of the programme.

When building up a free skating sequence, the use you make of the surface available is important too. Therefore spins and jumps should be distributed over the entire ice rink to avoid the impression of monotony. In a successful sequence, difficult parts should not come one after the other. Intersperse passages of steps between jumps and spins so as not to be skating from one start to the next. The movements of your skating and free legs are very important. Arm movements alone, however, should preferably be kept for ice show dancers. As far as jumps are concerned, height, speed, momentum and distance are the features of a good performance.

There are jumps with and without a number of rotations. At present, for example, world-class skaters try to master a triple Axel-Paulsen, ie a jump of three and a half rotations ($= 1260°$), in which you jump forwards and land backwards.

Classic windmill spin.

Neat straddle spin.

Variation of the windmill spin.

Well-controlled turning is a decisive factor in performing a spin correctly – and therefore the number of rotations and the speed. The body's centre of gravity for this must always be directly beneath the rotating skate.

There are two-foot and one-foot spins in which the latter are divided into standing, sit and camel spins. The rotations can be inside, outside, forward or backward. Moreover, you can perform change spins (from leg to position changes) with innumerable variations.

The steps must co-ordinate with the rhythm of the music, be full of momentum and be skated with gentle, flowing movements.

Short programme

But free skating is only the last stage of a championship, since the skater must previously have completed the generally tiresome compulsory section and a short programme, which must not exceed two minutes. This is concerned with free-skating moves consisting of four groups and have been laid down in advance for five years by the ISU (see page 126) Figure Skating Commission. There are seven moves in each, consisting of a double Axel-Paulsen, two jump combinations with either two double jumps or one double and a triple jump, a flying spin, a spin with a change of foot, a spin combination and a passage of steps. Skaters choose their own music. You cannot repeat movements you fail on or include additional jumps, spins or steps.

The short programme is judged openly with A and B marks (see page 123). The full free-skating programme has a section worth 50 percent and the short one amounts to 20 percent of the total available score.

For some years it has been possible to take examinations in free skating. The moves described above are divided into four classes and are marked by three judges.

Information on free skating

The free skating classes

Class IV
includes the following moves:
1. Three jump
2. Salchow
3. Rittberger
4. Thoren
5. Toe loop
6. Spreadeagle jump
7. Standing spin BI
8. Sit spin BI
9. Camel spin BI
10. Crossing in figure of eight over whole ice rink forward and backward
11. Three jumps in figure of eight with linking steps

Class III
includes the following moves:
1. Walley jump
2. One-foot Axel
3. Flip jump
4. Axel-Paulsen
5. Lutz jump
6. Double Salchow
7. Camel spin BO
8. Sit spin BO
9. Camel/sit spin BI
10. Choctaw steps in circular or serpentine shape
11. Mohawk steps in straight line

Class II
includes the following moves:
1. Spreadeagle Lutz
2. Double toe loop
3. Double Rittberger
4. 3 Walleys, one behind the other
5. Axel-Paulsen BI
6. Three jump – Rittberger – Thoren – Double Salchow
7. Flying sit spin BO
8. Flying camel spin BO
9. Change – sit spin (two changes)
10. Quick turn steps round a circle
11. Serpentine – looping – step in straight line

Class I
includes the following moves:
1. Axel-Paulsen BI – double Salchow
2. Axel-Paulsen – double toe loop
3. Double Axel-Paulsen
4. Double Lutz
5. Double flip jump
6. Three jump of free choice
7. Flying sit spin BI
8. Flying camel spin BO with a jump turn into a sit spin
9. Jump turn into a camel spin
10. Straight line step sequence in which compulsory moves (turns, counter-turns, Threes etc) can be recognized
11. Circular quick step sequence with recognizable main steps to both sides.

Information on free skating

	Three jump	½ turn from forward outside to backward outside
	Axel-Paulsen	1½ turns from forward outside to backward outside
	Double Axel-Paulsen	2½ turns from forward outside to backward outside
	Triple Axel-Paulsen	3½ turns from forward outside to backward outside
	Salchow	1 turn from backward inside to backward outside
	Double Salchow	2 turns from backward inside to backward outside
	Triple Salchow	3 turns from backward inside to backward outside
	Flip (dabbed Salchow)	1 turn dabbed from backward inside to backward outside
	Double flip (dabbed double Salchow)	2 turns dabbed from backward inside to backward outside
	Triple flip (dabbed triple Salchow)	3 turns dabbed from backward inside to backward outside
	Loop (Rittberger)	1 turn from backward outside to backward outside

The most common jumps

	Double loop (double Rittberger)	2 turns from backward outside to backward outside
	Triple loop (triple Rittberger)	3 turns from backward outside to backward outside
	Lutz	1 counter-turn from backward outside to backward outside
	Double Lutz	2 counter-turns from backward outside to backward outside
	Triple Lutz	3 counter-turns from backward outside to backward outside
	Spreadeagled jump	½ counter-turn with legs spreadeagled dabbed from backward outside to forward inside
	Spreadeagled Lutz	1 counter-turn with legs spreadeagled dabbed from backward outside to backward outside

Skating school I

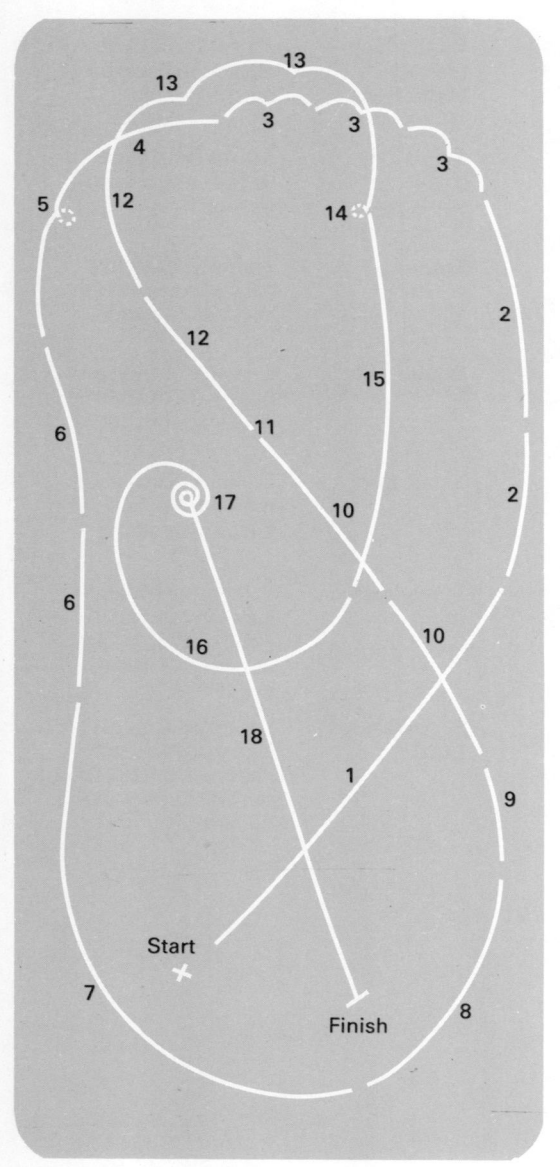

Example of free-skating programme

1 = preliminary steps
2 = loop 2×
3 = Three steps 3×
4 = backward – crossing over
5 = Three jump
6 = change steps 2×
7 = camel forward
8 = camel backward
9 = loop 1×
10 = Kilian step 2×
11 = tap jump
12 = backward change step 2×
13 = Three steps inwards 2×
14 = Three jump
15 = double-time steps forward
16 = moon
17 = two-foot spin
18 = camel forward

Skating school II

Example of free-skating programme

1 = preliminary steps
2 = one-foot spin BI
3 = backward crossover
4 = toe loop
5 = forward crossover
6 = moon
7 = preliminary steps
8 = tap jump
9 = change steps forward 3×
10 = camel forward
11 = loop 2×
12 = camel spin
13 = Kilian step
14 = moon Salchow
15 = backward double-time steps
16 = Three jump
17 = Three jumps inside 2×
18a = start for
18 = sit spin
19 = Three steps 3×
20 = Salchow
21 = backward crossover
22 = scissor jump
23 = change step backward 2×
24 = camel backward
25 = Three steps 2×
26 = toe loop
27 = sideways hopping
28 = Three forward inside
29 = camel/sit spin

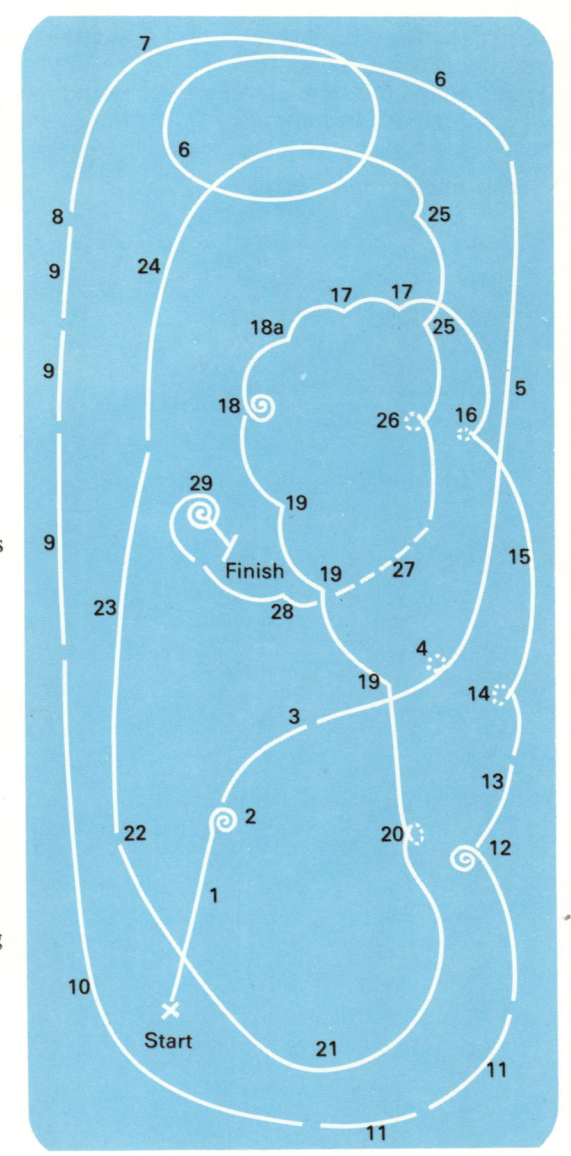

Information

Curve skating is the basic prerequisite for the mastery of spins, jumps and steps as well as dancing moves. In compulsory skating the 'layout' of the figure is particularly important. The skater thereby shows a feeling for the geometrical shape of the

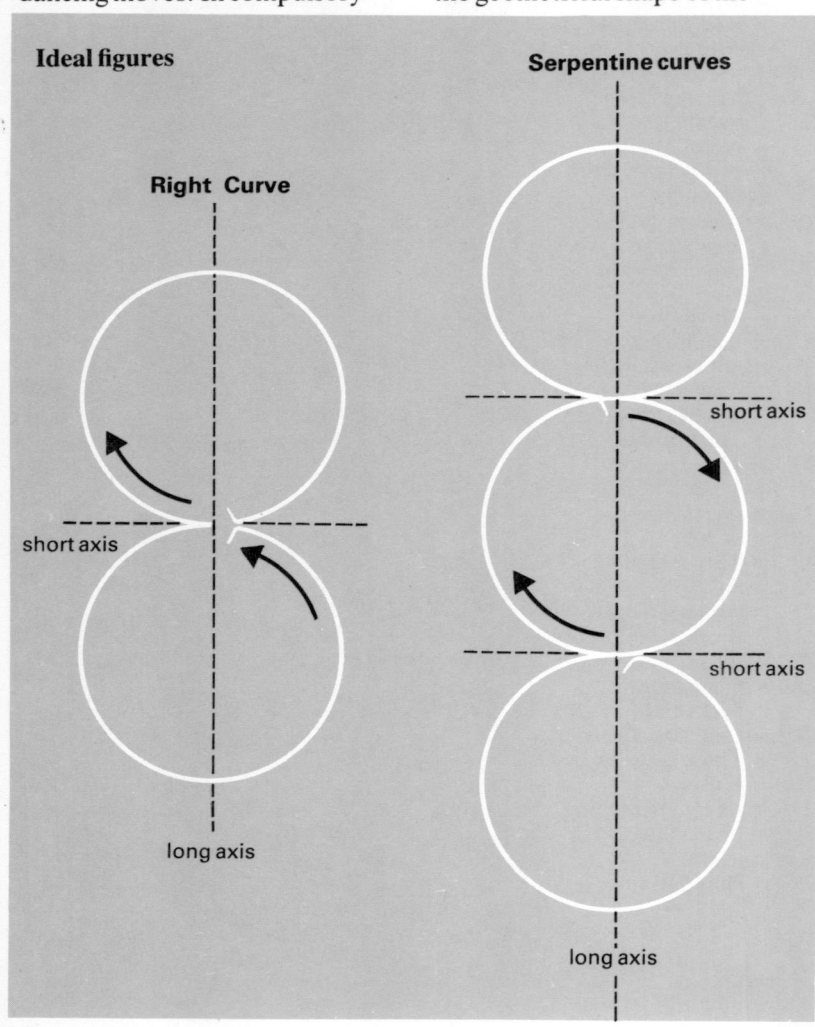

Ideal figures

Right Curve

short axis

long axis

Serpentine curves

short axis

short axis

long axis

on compulsory skating

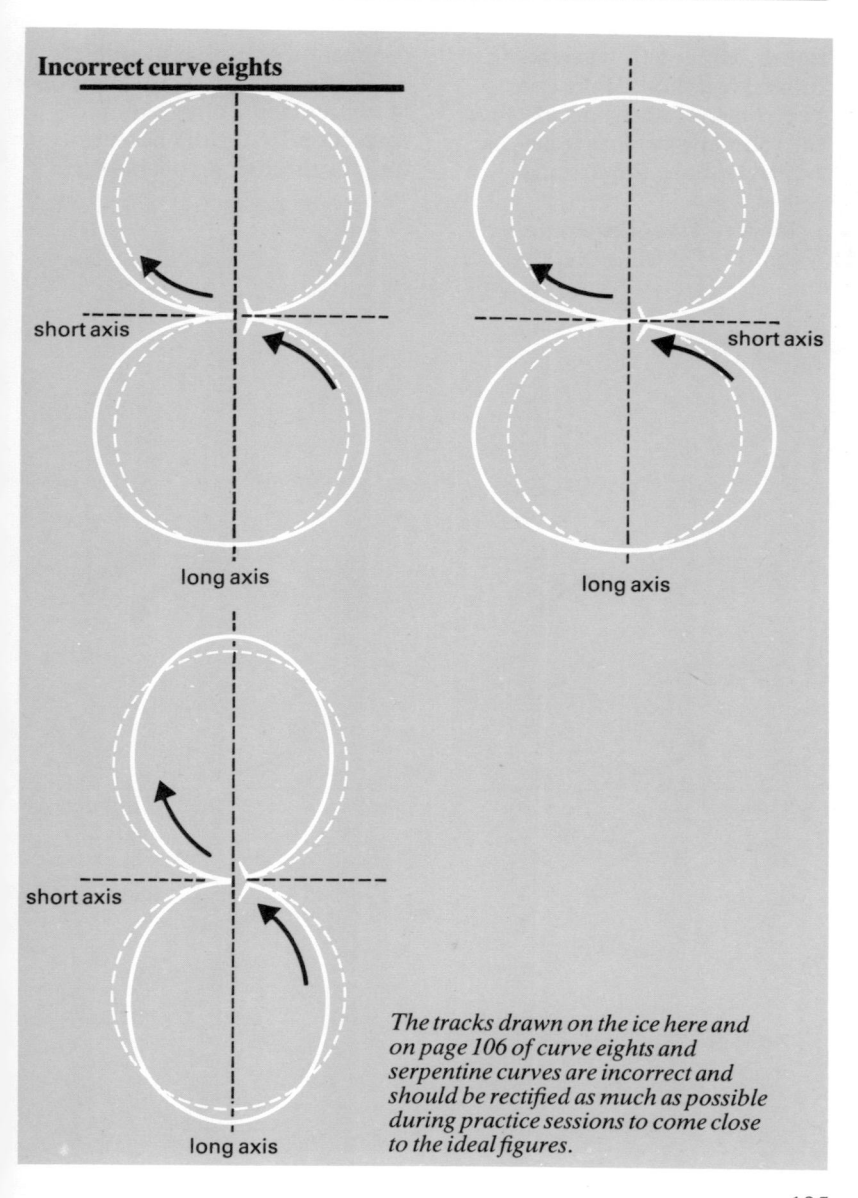

Incorrect curve eights

short axis

long axis

short axis

long axis

short axis

long axis

The tracks drawn on the ice here and on page 106 of curve eights and serpentine curves are incorrect and should be rectified as much as possible during practice sessions to come close to the ideal figures.

Information

figure. Moreover, when being judged you should take care to keep the long and short axes and the roundness of the circles, as well as to make the size and proportion of the figure agree.

The size of each figure in curves of two and three circles should correspond to the diameter of roughly three times the height of

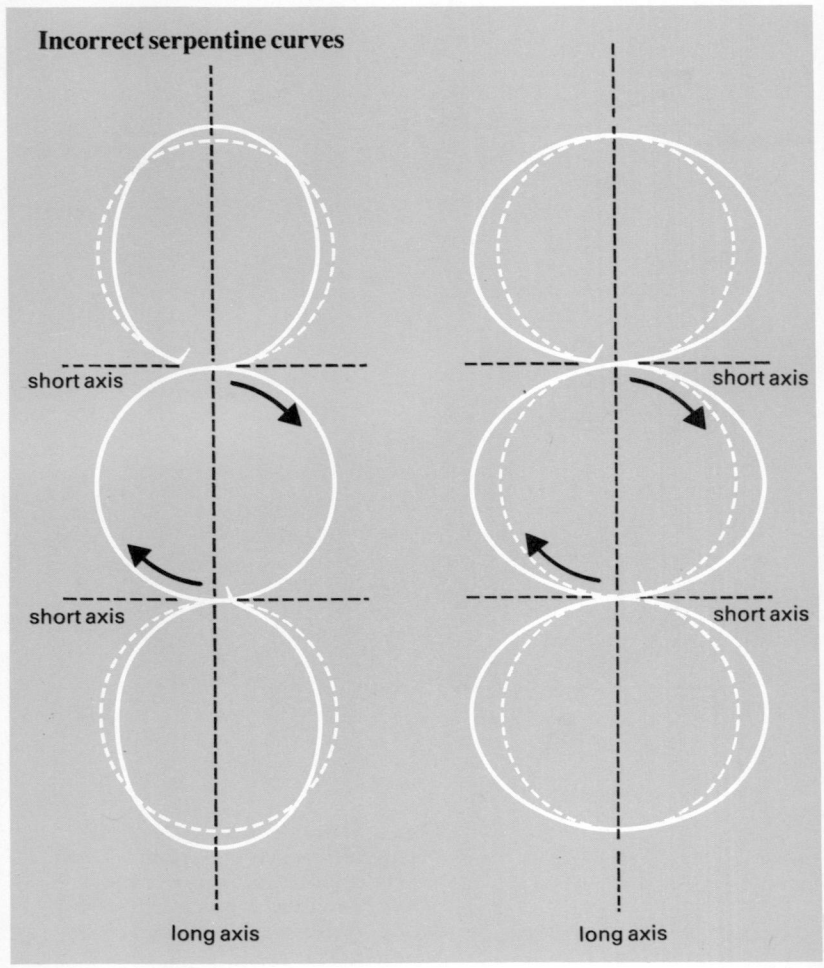

Incorrect serpentine curves

on compulsory skating

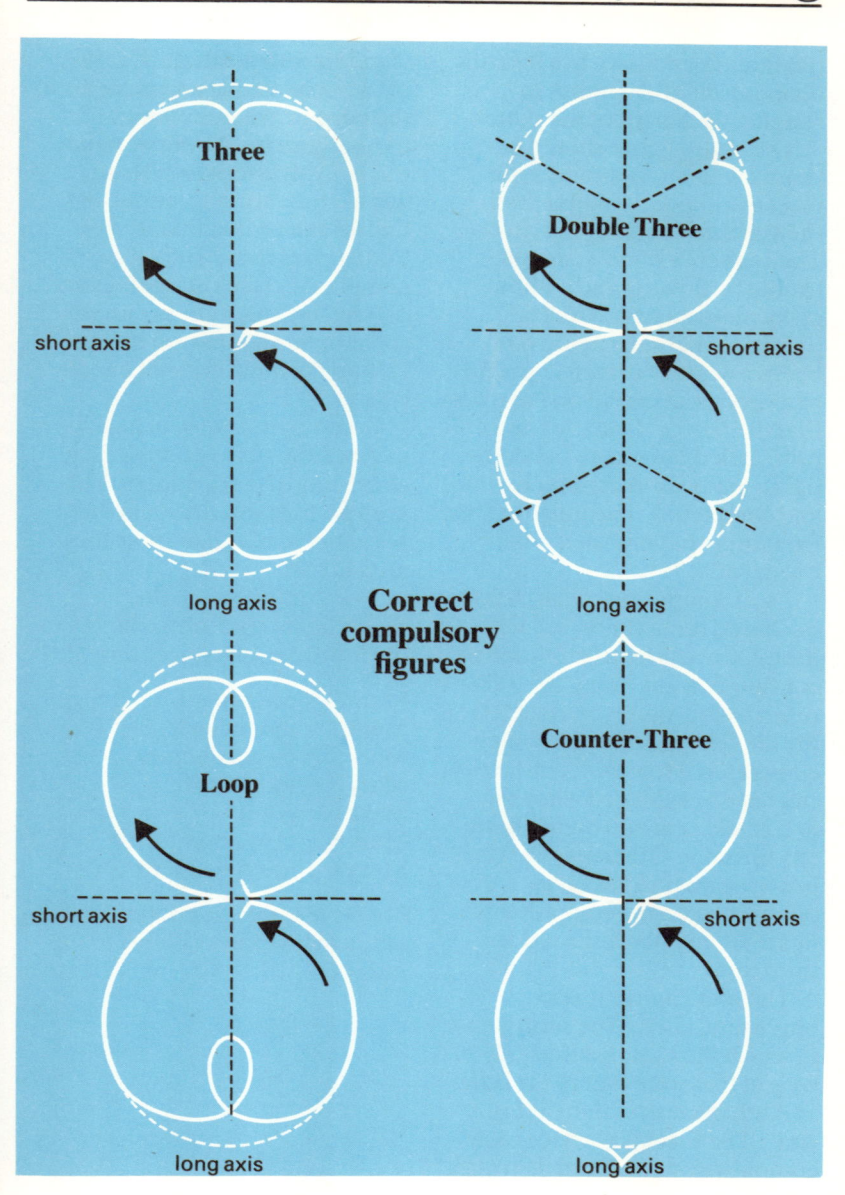

Three

Double Three

short axis

short axis

long axis

Correct compulsory figures

Loop

Counter-Three

short axis

short axis

long axis

long axis

Information on compulsory skating

the skater per circle. In a loop the diameter should amount to roughly the height of the skater.

The entire figure should be skated with momentum at the most even speed possible from the start to the end of the circle. The sequence of movements should be flowing and without jerky movements. With the judging, whether a figure has been executed correctly depends to a very great extent on the track that the skater leaves on the ice (also called the sketch) after the figure has been skated three times and completed. The judge can see from this what mistakes have been made.

Each compulsory figure has to be skated three times on each foot. Devote a lot of attention to continuity when doing this. This refers to the 'unity' of track left on the ice after the figure has been completed. However, continuity can only be achieved when the first track is carried out without any mistake. Otherwise the track has to be rectified as far as possible when the compulsory figure is repeated a second and third time.

The foot change is also important. This is the short phase in which the skater shifts body weight from one foot to the other.

And, of course, there is the start. The first take-off for each compulsory figure is made from a standing-still position. The take-off must be strong and made from the edge to achieve enough momentum for the entire figure. Pushing off afterwards is not allowed. Learning compulsory figures can be documented by taking class tests. The 41 compulsory steps altogether are divided into four classes, in which the simplest figures are in Class IV and the most difficult ones in Class I.

In championships, one group is drawn from three groups, each consisting of three figures. The group which was drawn in the previous year's championship is missed out.

The judging conforms roughly to the following classifications:

Mark 0 = not skated
Mark 1 = inadequate
Mark 2 = unsatisfactory
Mark 3 = moderate
Mark 4 = good
Mark 5 = very good
Mark 6 = faultless, perfect

For further differentiation, tenths of full marks are available to the judges.

Compulsory figures

The compulsory figures

R = right	O = outside		Rk = rocker
L = left	I = inside		Br = bracket
F = forward	T = Three		C = counter
B = backward	Lp = loop		

Figure	No	Name	Description
	1a	**Curve**	RFO, LFO
	b	**eight**	LFO, RFO
	2a		RFI, LFI
	b		LFI, RFI
	3a		RBO, LBO
	b		LBO, RBO
	4a		RBI, LBI
	b		LBI, RBI
	5a	**Change**	RFOI, LBIO
	b		LFOI, RFIO
	6a		RBOI, LBIO
	b		LBOI, RBIO
	7a	**Three**	RFOTBI, LFOTBI
	b		LFOTBI, RFOTBI
	8a		RFOTBI, LFITFO
	b		LFOTBI, RBITFO
	9a		RFITBO, LBOTFI
	b		LFITBO, RBOTFI
	10a	**Double Three**	RFOTBITFO, LFOTBITFO
	b		LFOTBITFO, RFOTBITFO
	11a		RFITBOTFI, LFITBOTFI
	b		LFITBOTFI, RFITBOTFI
	12a		RBOTFITBO, LBOTFITBO
	b		LBOTFITBO, RBOTFITBO
	13a		RBITFOTBI, LBITFOTBI
	b		LBITFOTBI, RBITFOTBI

Information on compulsory skating

Figure	No	Name	Description
	14a	**Loop**	RFOLpFO, LFOLpFO
	b		LFOLpFO, RFOLpFO
	15a		RFILpFl, LFILpFl
	b		LFILpFl, RFILpFl
	16a		RBOLpBO, LBOLpBO
	b		LBOLpBO, RBOLpBO
	17a		RBILpBl, LBILpBl
	b		LBILpBl, RBILpBl
	18a	**Bracket**	RFOBrBl, LBIBrFO
	b		LFOBrBl, RBIBrFO
	19a		RFIBrBO, LBOBrFl
	b		LFIBrBO, RBOBrFl
	20a	**Rocker**	RFORkBO, LBORkFO
	b		LFORkBO, RBORkFO
	21a		RFIRkBl, LBIRkFl
	b		LFIRkBl, RBIRkFl
	22a	**Counter**	RFOCBO, LBOCFO
	b		LFOCBO, RBOCFO
	23a		RFICBl, LBICFl
	b		LFICBl, RBICFl
	24a	**One-foot eight**	RFOI, LFIO
	b		LFOI, RFIO
	25a		RBOI, LBIO
	b		LBOI, RBIO

Compulsory figures

Figure	No	Name	Description
	26a b 27a b	**Change Three**	RFOITBO, LBOITFO LFOITBO, RBOITFO RFIOTBI, LBIOTFI LFIOTBI, RBIOTFI
	28a b 29a b	**Change – double Three**	RFOITBOTFI, LFIOTBITFO LFOITBOTFI, RFIOTBOTFO RBOITFOTBI, LBIOTFITBO LBOITFOTBI, RBIOTFITBO
	30a b 31a b	**Change loop**	RFOILpFI, LFIOLpFO LFOILpFI, RFIOLpFO RBOILpBI, LBIOLpBO LBOILpBI, RBIOLpBO
	32a b 33a b	**Change bracket**	RFOIBrBO, LBOIBrFO LFOIBrBO, RBOIBrFO RFIOBrBI, LBIOBrFI LFIOBrBI, RBIOBrFI

Information on compulsory skating

Figure	No	Name	Description
	34a	**Paragraph**	RFOTBIOTFI, LFITBOITFO
	b	**Three**	LFOTBIOTFI, RFITBOITFO
	35a		RBOTFIOITBI, LBITFOITBO
	b		LBOTFIOTBI, RBITFOITBO
	36a	**Paragraph double Three**	RFOTBITFOITBOTFI-LFITBOTFIOTBITFO
	b		LFOTBITFOITBOTFI-RFITBOTFIOTBITFO
	37a		RBOTFITBOITFOTBI-LBITFOTBIOTFITBO
	b		LBOTFITBOITFOTBI-RBITFOTBIOTFITBO
	38a	**Paragraph loop**	RFOLpOILpI, LFILpIOLpFO
	b		LFOLpFOILpI, RFILpIOLpFO
	39a		RBOLpBOILpI, LBILpIOLpBO
	b		LBOLpOILpI, RBILpBIOLpBO
	40a	**Paragraph bracket**	RFOBrBIOBrFI, LFIBrBOIBrFO
	b		LFOBrBIOBrFI, RFIBrBIOBrFO
	41a		RBOBrFIOBrBI, LBIBrFOIBrBO
	b		LBOBrFIOBrBI, RBIBrFOIBrBO

The class tests

Class skating test IV:
Compulsory figures nos 1, 2, 3, 5, 7, 9, 10, 11, 12, 28.

Class skating test III:
Compulsory figures nos 4, 6, 8, 13, 14, 15, 18, 19, 24, 26, 30.

Class skating test II:
Compulsory figures nos 16, 17, 22, 23, 25, 27, 29, 32, 33, 34, 35.

Class skating test I:
Compulsory figures nos 20, 21, 31, 36, 37, 38, 39a+b, 40, 41a+b.

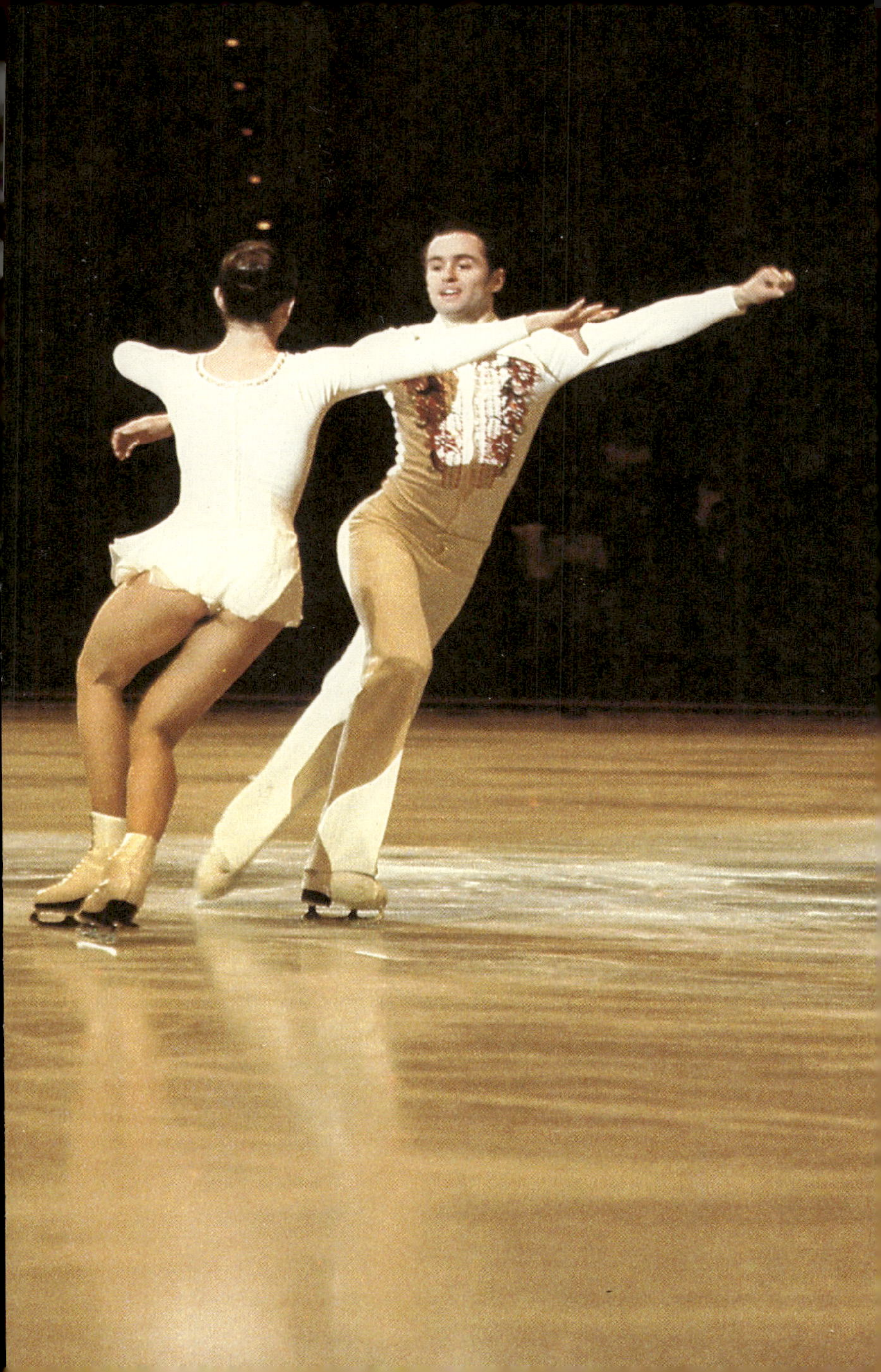

Information

As in compulsory skating you can take dancing tests in ice dancing too. These tests are divided into three classes. In the third class you skate three dances and six dances in the second class. In the first class, besides six compulsory dances, the skater also has to carry out an original set dance as well as a free dance lasting four minutes.

Compulsory dances

Whereas the music for the compulsory dances (there are 18 in all) is chosen by the appropriate judge, the examinees choose their own music for the original set dance and the free dance.

When carrying out compulsory dances ensure that the tracks made in one dance signify the sketch of a whole step sequence on the ice. Therefore, there are dances with 'predescribed tracks' and 'preferred tracks'. There is also the 'edge dance'.

Original set dance

The rhythm and tempo limit for this dance is laid down two years in advance by the ISU.

The original set dance should not be a free dance, although the music is chosen by the couple themselves. Contrary to the free dance the original set dance must

Free dance figure: harmony of movement and music comes to the fore.

be made up of step sequences (to be repeated), which in length amount to either the whole perimeter of the ice rink or half of it. The choice of steps, turns and step combinations is free. Only steps using the points of your skates are prohibited.

The aim when putting together an original set dance is to perform difficult moves within the character of the dance and the musical rhythm. As far as possible it should not be a dance that is similar to the compulsory dances (see **Tango** example on pages 116/7).

on ice dancing

The harmony is hard to work out in dancing moves.

The free dance

Here there are no predescribed step sequences and as far as possible no repetitive passages. It should bear no similarity to a pair-skating free dance. The music is freely chosen by the couple themselves. However, it must be dance music that is suited in its rhythm and tempo to ice dancing. Also the section should consist at the most of three different pieces of music. The free dance lasts four minutes in championships.

In the free dance the gymnastic aspect should come to the fore. Therefore arabesques (camels) and pivots are allowed that do not exceed a specified time. Spins should not be of more than three revolutions and lifts are only allowed if the man does not prop up the woman, ie his arm does not stretch above her waist. Also one and a half revolutions at the most are allowed. Small jumps are possible, too, when a partner changes feet or direction. But only half a turn is allowed.

The ice-dancing tests

Ice-dancing tests are divided into three classes:

Class III = Bronze Test
European waltz
Foxtrot
Fourteen

Class II = Silver Test
American waltz
Rocker foxtrot
Blues
Kilian
Starlight waltz
Tango

Class I = Gold Test
Paso doble
Argentinian tango
Quickstep
Vienna waltz
Rumba
Westminster waltz
Original set dance
4-minute free dance

Information

Original set dance
Example: tango

You can use the diagram shown on the right as an example for working out an original set dance.

This tango, also called the Harris tango so as not to be confused with the Argentinian tango, was first performed in public in London in 1932. It was invented by Paul Kreckow and Trudy Harris. It has been in the standard repertoire of compulsory dances for many years. If you want to take the Silver Test, you must learn this tango. In the meantime, many original set dances of former skaters have been taken over and become essential parts of the compulsory dance repertoire. Dances are valid and can be recognized and skated as original set dances only when their inventors no longer take an active part in championships and competitions.

Women's steps

1 = crossed behind LBO	beat 1
2 = crossed Chassé RFI	1
3 = LBO	4
4 = crossed behind RBO	1
5 = crossed Chassé LBI	1
6 = RBO	4
7 = crossed behind LBO	2
8 = RFO	1
9 = crossed Chassé LFI	1
10 = RFO	4
11 = crossed in front LFO	1
12 = crossed Chassé RFI	1
13 = LFO	4
14 = crossed counter curve RFO Three to RBI	1
15 = LBO	1
16 = RFI	4
17 = LFO	1
18 = RFI	2
19 = LFO	2
20 = RFO swing curve } closed	4
21 = LBO swing curve } Mohawk	4
22 = RFI Three	1
to RBO	5

Men's steps

1 = crossed in front RFO	beat 1
2 = crossed Chassé LFI	1
3 = RFO	4
4 = crossed in front LFO	1
5 = crossed Chassé RFI	1
6 = LFO	4
7 = crossed in front RFO to rocker RO	1+1
8 = crossed behind LBO	1
9 = crossed Chassé RBI	1
10 = LBO	4
11 = crossed behind RBO	1
12 = crossed Chassé LBI	1
13 = RBO	4
14 = crossed counter curve LBO	2
15 = RFO	4
16 = LFO	1
17 = RFI	1
18 = LFO	2
19 = double-time step RFI	2
20 = LFI swing curve } closed	4
21 = RBI swing curve } Mohawk	4
22 = LFO	1
Chassé RFI	1
LFO	4

on ice dancing

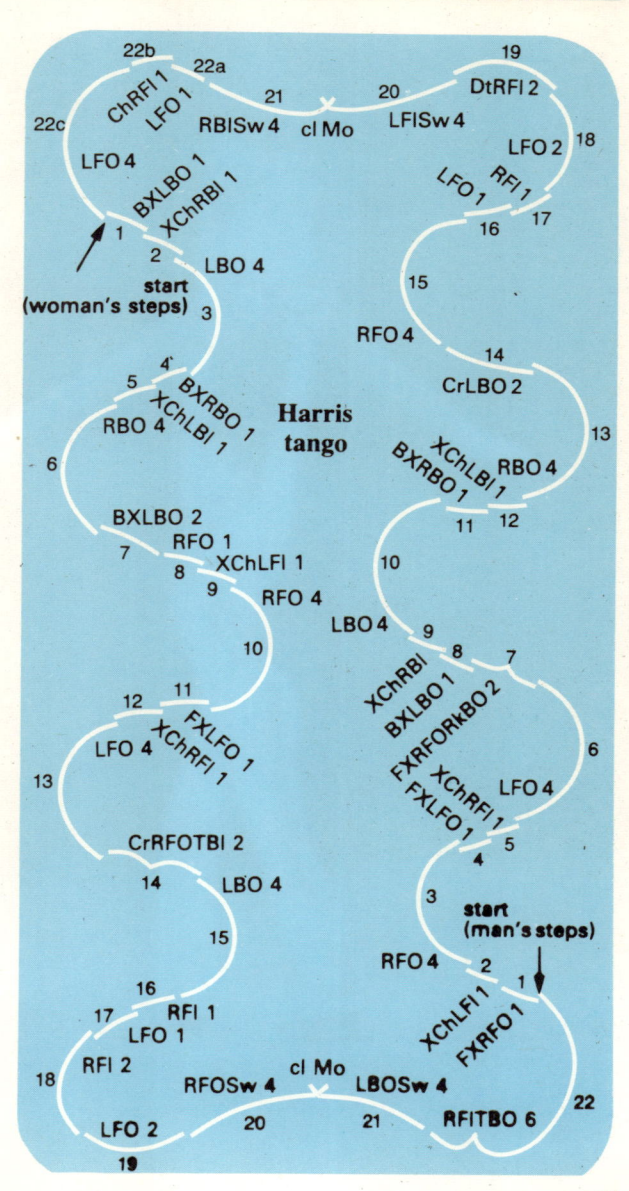

Harris tango

woman's steps (start at 1)

- 1 BXLBO 1
- 2 XChRBI 1
- 3 LBO 4
- 4 BXRBO 1
- 5 XChLBI 1
- 6 RBO 4
- 7 BXLBO 2
- 8 RFO 1
- 9 XChLFI 1
- 10 RFO 4
- 11 FXLFO 1
- 12 XChRFI 1
- 13 LFO 4
- 14 CrRFOTBI 2
- 15 LBO 4
- 16 RFI 1
- 17 LFO 1
- 18 RFI 2
- 19 LFO 2
- 20 RFOSw 4
- 21 cl Mo
- 22a RBISw 4
- 22b ChRFI 1
- 22c LFO 1 / LFO 4

man's steps (start at 1)

- 1 FXRFO 1
- 2 XChLFI 1
- 3 RFO 4
- 4 FXLFO 1
- 5 XChRFI 1
- 6 LFO 4
- 7 FXRFORkBO 2
- 8 BXLBO 1
- 9 XChRBI
- 10 LBO 4
- 11 BXRBO 1
- 12 XChLBI 1
- 13 RBO 4
- 14 CrLBO 2
- 15 RFO 4
- 16 LFO 1
- 17 RFI 1
- 18 LFO 2
- 19 DtRFI 2
- 20 LFISw 4
- 21 cl Mo
- 22 LBOSw 4 / RFITBO 6

117

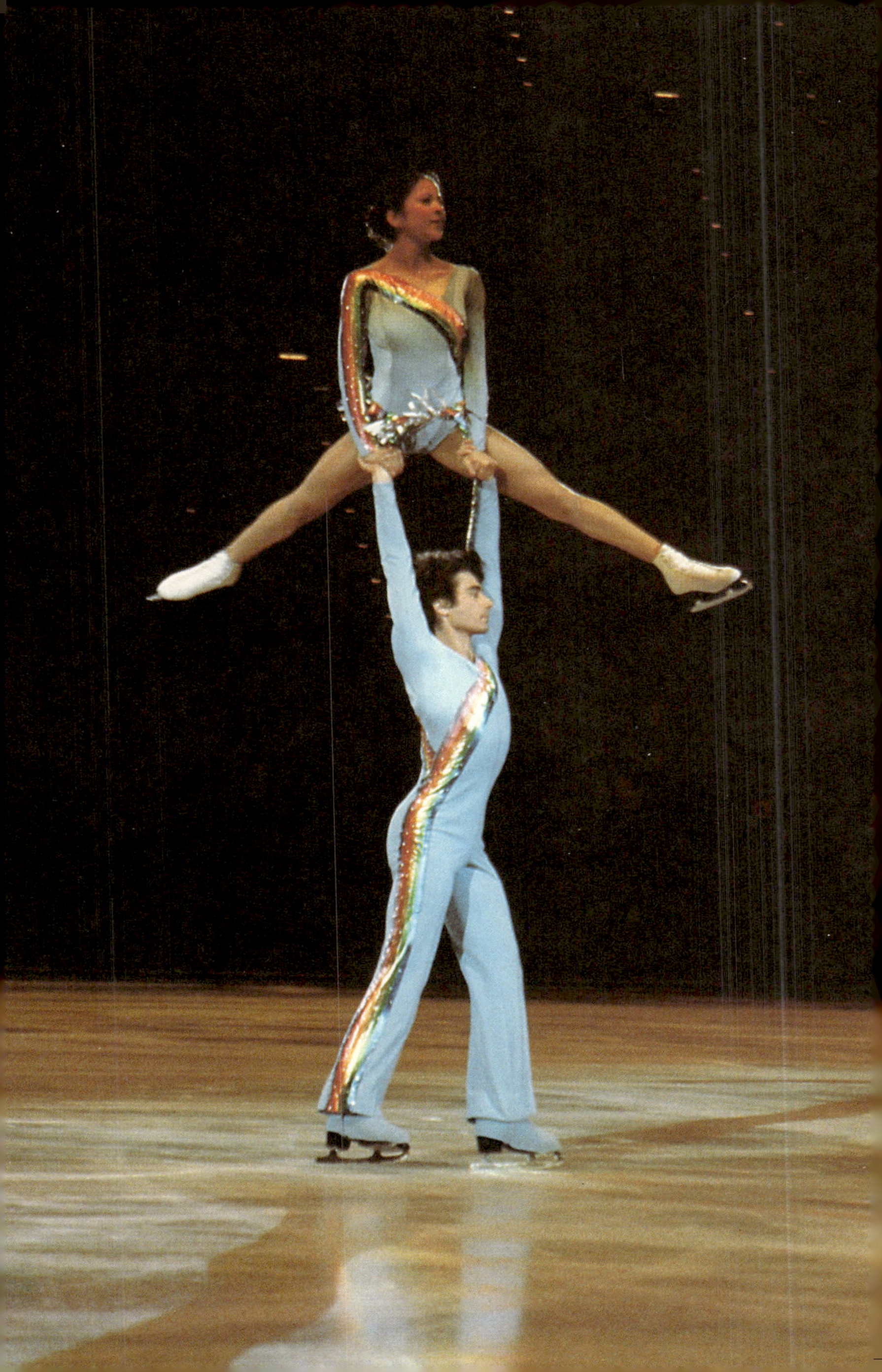

Information on pair skating

In pair skating there is no compulsory skating but a short programme. But since they can only perform the free-skating moves when they have learned the basic forms of the compulsory figures, pair skaters must also spend time doing compulsory training.

Of course no female or male skaters begin as pair skaters, but always as singles skaters. To be able to perform the simplest pair-skating figures presupposes a good grounding in singles skating.

Harmony in pair skating

Readiness to adapt is important for a pair and one skater's style should also harmonize with that of the partner. The direction of travel should also agree with the performance of the free-skating moves. The pair should match each other as far as possible in size and the age difference should not be too great since a skater's maturity depends on age.

In championships pair skating is composed of the short programme and the free skating. The music is chosen by the pair for both performances, and unlimited sections are allowed. It is only important that the pair's music is converted into corresponding moves.

Even when the partners are performing different figures, a harmonious impression should still be given.

Short programme

As in championships, we will start with the short programme, which should not exceed two minutes. It consists of six elements stipulated in detail beforehand. These were laid down in four groups by the ISU and are drawn five years in advance. The short programme can turn out to be even shorter, as long as all the moves are contained in it. A failed figure cannot be repeated in pair skating, either.

A double jump (each skater makes a solo jump) is contained in the four groups. Also included

Information

is a lift with a double turn, a death spiral, a pair-skating spin and a solo spin (to be turned separately), as well as a passage of steps stipulated in their layout.

The short programme is openly marked and judged with two sets of marks. In the first set of marks the technical merit of the stipulated moves is judged, whereas the second set reflects the artistic impression.

Classical pair-skating figure: the lady's death spiral and the man's pivot.

Pair-skating free section

A pair-skating free section in championships lasts five minutes and demands a high degree of fitness, especially from the man so that he still has reserves of strength left for lifts in the final minute.

A good programme also contains solo skating by both partners in which they perform passages either symmetrically (mirror skating) or parallel to one another (shadow skating). Of course there are also the typical pair-skating figures such as lifts, camels, spirals and spins, which

on pair skating

are harmoniously completed by steps and dancing moves. Neither partner should constantly skate the same figures and both can separate from time to time. However, the overall impression of agreement and harmony in the partners' performance must be guaranteed.

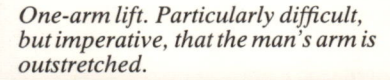

One-arm lift. Particularly difficult, but imperative, that the man's arm is outstretched.

Pair-skating sit spin: Tscherkessen spin.

Lifts

For lifts, there are definite rules that state that the female partner has to jump by herself and can only be supported by her partner with certain holds (hand-to-hand, hand-to-arm and hand-to-body), but never by the legs. To perform a lift successfully, it is important for the man's arms to be stretched out completely and not kept at shoulder height. There are also two and one-armed lifts.

Judging in the pair-skating free section is also carried out openly and is likewise made up of two sets of marks.

Rules and marking

All championship and competition rules are laid down in the Competition Rules for Figure Skating (WOK). There you can look up who is an amateur, what prerequisites in ice skating the participant in a championship has to fulfil, how advertisements for events have to look, what qualifications a judge and referee must have and what duties they must perform, how a team of judges is made up and the principles of judging.

Judging
Whereas previously the compulsory section amounted to two-thirds of the marks and the free section only one third, the relationship between the free and compulsory sections has been basically altered for some time. Also a new aid for fairer marking has come about; that is the short programme for singles skaters and pairs and the original set dance for dancers.

In singles skating, compulsory figures marks now make up 30 percent of the entire result and a further 20 percent for the short programme, so that the free section now has a 50 percent share of the final result. This change ensured that those skaters who did well only in the compulsory section were not necessarily placed among the leaders if they hadn't done well overall in their performance.

In ice-dancing championships, the marks are allocated as follows: 30 percent of the whole result is allotted to the compulsory dances, 20 percent to the original set dance and the free dancing carries 50 percent of the final marking.

In pairs the performance of the short programme has a 40 percent share in the whole result. The rest is made up from the free skating.

Open marking
Championships basically use the open marking system, ie using marking boxes or an electronic indicator board. The judge keeps a record of all his marks previously quoted and, before the marks appear, he has to give a note of his marks to the referee. In this way belated corrections or alterations to marks to suit those of the other judges in the team are avoided.

Secret marking
In compulsory skating, as in championships, the open marking system is used, while in class skating tests and dancing tests at the association level a secret marking system is used. Here the judge just writes his marks on a record sheet. He only learns himself at the end of the test how he has marked a skater in relation to his fellow judges. This

Rules and marking

makes skaters nervous as they do not know right away, as in the open marking, how their performance has been rated.

Compulsory figures and compulsory dances are only given one set of marks, which includes the whole performance of the figure/dance. In the original set dance, two sets of marks are given:

Mark A
The first mark (**A**) judges the arrangement as well as originality, degree of difficulty and correct repetition of the step sequence.

Mark B
The second mark (**B**) expresses the rating of the presentation, such as the pair's movement to the musical rhythm, how the dance makes use of the ice and flowing style.

Technical merit
In free dancing **Mark A** is used for the technical merit, ie the degree of difficulty of the figures presented, the variety and sureness of the performance.

Artistic impression
Mark B expresses the artistic impression, such as whether the programme has been put together harmoniously, use of space, whether the moves flow to the musical rhythm and originality of ideas. In the short and free programmes in singles and pair skating, two sets of marks are likewise given. **Mark A** is for technical merit, the degree of difficulty of the performance, the variety of moves as well as sureness. **Mark B** rates the music or musicality of the performances and the make-up of the free section in relation to spatial circumstances and the expression of the dancing. In pair skating the harmony of moves is also marked. In championships the judging team generally consists of seven, with a referee. In class skating tests and dancing tests, three judges mark the tests in each case.

Judges
The judges themselves are, as a rule, former skaters, but they do not necessarily have to have taken part in national or international championships. However, all aspiring judges have to take suitability tests to prove that not only do they know how difficult a figure is, but can also rate specific mistakes in relation to it. Also judges are not automatically 'promoted', but have to rise in the hierarchy of judges on merit. But, at the same time, this means that judges are subject to supervision when they serve, first at association level and

Rules and marking

then in national competitions – and later, after they have proved themselves, international ones too. We shall not discuss here the so-called 'nations marking'. But one thing still deserves mention. A team of judges with differing marks does not accurately reflect a skater's ability. Only by comparing the marks of an individual judge in relation to all the skaters can an individual skater's ability be properly assessed.

To reach a common starting point for marking a discipline, the competition judges mostly discuss among themselves before the championship begins or often briefly after the first skater has performed. But if you believe that marks are then fixed or arranged, you are wrong. It is here only a question of an approximate agreement of opinions. This does not harm the skater in any way. The main thing is that each judge then continues marking the skaters consistently in relation to this.

Between two winters

Even the longest winter finally comes to an end. Lakes are once again being used for water sports and outdoor ice stadiums close at the end of March until October.

If you do not want to give up skating in summer, you should change to roller skates. The four wheels under each foot offer more of a surface to stand on and more stability. At the beginning, and for those trying it out for the first time, roller skates with rubber or plastic wheels are enough. But you should in all cases wear boots to give your feet the firmest possible support. Never fix roller skates on to rubber boots or shoes. There are also special skating sets, which are considerably dearer to buy but do give more stability. Many ice-skating associations have a roller-skating department and corresponding roller-skating rinks. You can also join separate roller-skating clubs. Multi-purpose sports halls can be used for roller skating. Any asphalt surface will do as well if it is not impeded by traffic, if it is not sloping and if it does not have any small stones, cracks, grooves or other uneven parts. Otherwise the wheels would get stuck and the skater would fall. And a fall on to asphalt is more painful than one on to ice. You do not, therefore, necessarily have to resort to the disco floor for your first attempts on roller skates to keep fit for the following winter.

On roller skates the figures can look just as elegant.

Glossary of terms

Artificial ice Ice surface with coils set into the floor to freeze the ice.

Beginning Start of the season.

Blade The hollow-ground gliding runner of the skate with toe rakes (picks) for figure skating.

Butterfly Solo jump developed from the Three jump. Your body lies as horizontally as possible in the air.

Camel Skating figure in singles and pair skating.

Chassé Figure skating step.

Choctaw Dance step.

Choreography Spatial distribution and arrangement of the free programme made up of jumps, spins and steps as well as dancing moves.

Class skating test Altogether 41 compulsory figures divided into four tests. These are taken as proof that the figures have been learnt.

Compulsory dance Dance with stipulated or preferred track pictures or laid out as circular dance.

Continuity Every compulsory figure is skated three times on each foot. The circles traced on the ice should lie one on top of the other as far as possible, ie cover one another.

Dance tests 15 out of 18 compulsory dances, divided into three classes, are to be taken in the test.

Death spiral Pair skating figure with many variations.

Diagram Precise instructions and description of the layout of individual steps in ice dancing in relation to the ice surface.

Double track Incorrect tracing of a compulsory figure. Both edges become visible.

Drawing The track seen on the ice in compulsory figures.

Free dance Step combinations, but not passages of steps, made up from single compulsory dances. Free choice of music; lifts, higher jumps and distinctive spins are inadmissible.

Free skating Free programme arrangement consisting of spins, jumps, steps and dancing moves.

Guard Protector made of plastic for the runner when the blade is not on the ice.

Hollow-ground Special edge grinding for ice skates on the inner and outer edge.

ISU International Skating Union, umbrella association for the national ice-skating associations.

Ice show Arrangement without competition, but with theatrical elements.

Jump combination Several jumps one after the other.

Jumping leg The leg with which you take off.

Jumps Possible with and without turning. Most frequent ones are Three, Axel-Paulsen (1-3 times), Salchow (1-3 times), flip (1-3 times), loop or Rittberger (1-3 times), Lutz (1-3 times), toe loop with toe dug in on take-off (1-3 times).

Lifts Pair-skating moves; two and one-armed with one or more revolutions.

Loop Basic step in ice skating; also compulsory figure.

Glossary of terms

Mark A Technical merit; made up of difficulty, variety and sureness of performance.

Mark B Artistic impression; includes musicality, originality of ideas, spatial distribution of the performance and dancing expression. In pair skating the harmony of the moves as well.

Mohawk Dance step.

Moon Figure-skating figure in the shape of a moon.

Natural ice An ice rink sprayed with water or a frozen lake.

Open marking Judges pull their marks out of a marking box visible to everyone, or an electronic indicator board is used.

Overturning No correct finish to the jump. Momentum is not checked and the skater turns forward too early.

Paragraph Compulsory skating figure.

Pivot Skating figure in singles and pair skating.

Pureness of edge Criterion for marking a compulsory figure.

Running in Warming up to loosen muscles.

Secret marking Marks are written on record sheets only by the judges.

Short programme Moves stipulated in singles and pair skating according to the free choice of music.

Slip Slipping away when starting off or getting up momentum because of bad placement of weight when changing the skating leg.

Spin Two or one-foot revolutions on the ice with innumerable combinations and variations.

Spreadeagled jump Splits in the air.

Synchronized skating The pairs carry out the same moves singly beside one another.

Tapping (tapped) Touching the ground with your foot after a one-foot landing.

Team of judges National and international in championships; consisting of seven judges and one referee.

Three Step/turn in compulsory skating, free skating and in ice dancing.

Toe rakes Notches at the front of each blade.

Track picture dance Step sequence invented by dancing pair themselves with music chosen freely with stipulated rhythm.

Wandering Spin not centred. Your body's centre of gravity does not lie over your rotating skate.